Reengineering Business Processes And People Systems

Other Books By QualTeam

Continuous Improvement: Teams & Tools
by Robert F. Lynch and Thomas J. Werner

The Consultant's Handbook
by Thomas J. Werner and Robert F. Lynch

Reengineering Business Processes And People Systems

Robert F. Lynch

Thomas J. Werner

Published by

QualTeam, Inc.

5125 South Kipling Street, Suite 301
Littleton, CO 80127
(303) 972-1887

Acknowledgments

We would like to dedicate this book to the forward-thinking leaders we have known who started reinventing processes and people systems before the term "reengineering" was coined. Charlie Frenette and Amy White of The Coca-Cola Company, and Sheila Lambert, Howard Kiedaisch and Frank Platarote of Moody's Investors Service are these kinds of leaders.

We would like to thank Dr. Livia Lynch for her advice and commentary on this work. We very much appreciate the artistic expertise of Bob Clark of Studio Grafika. Finally, we are very grateful to Sallie Johnston for her administrative excellence, Tim Wojtalik for his graphic talents, Kim Greenway for PageMaker layout, and Ellen Galanty for her peerless proofreading and editing.

ISBN 0-9633398-2-6

Table of Contents

1

The Era Of Total Value

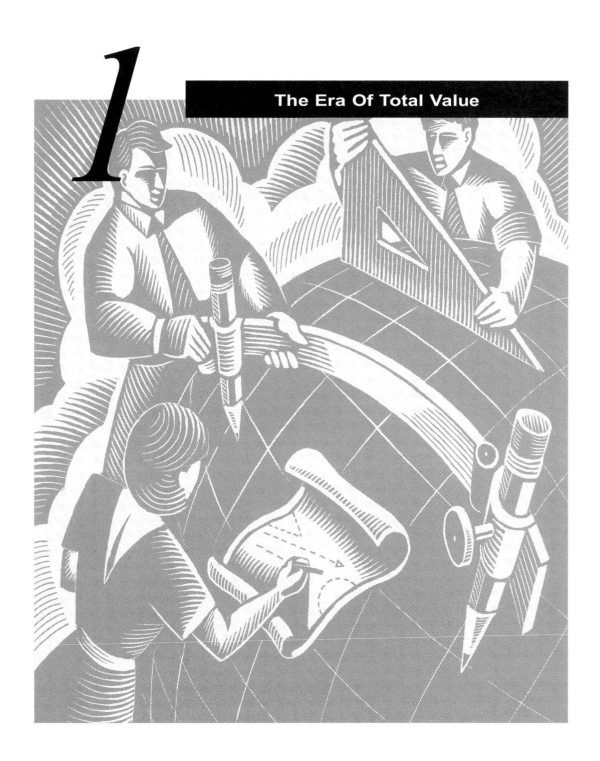

1

The New Era

The Limits Of The Quality Paradigm

The Mission Of This Book

Changing Large Organizations

The Era Of Total Value

Business has changed dramatically over the past two decades. While many businesses have adopted a total quality system in response to rising competition and increased consumer demand for quality, new business drivers have emerged, changing the game once again. These new drivers require another class of responses. Many businesses are changing enough to stay even but not enough to get ahead. When the 1980s ushered in the era of continuous quality improvement, we said, "Change never stops," and the 1990s have confirmed that with wave after wave of changes looming on the horizon.

The difficult truth today is that just when you have accomplished the change, the outside world can change faster and render your progress obsolete. What may be required is not the continuous improvement of a current system but the creation of an entirely new system based on a new set of operating rules.

One way to understand today's realities is to recognize the waves of change as a new era. We are moving from the era in which quality and customer service emerged as competitive responses to the business drivers of the 1980s to an era where these characteristics are givens and *total value* is the necessary competitive response. In this era of total value, competitiveness depends upon the ability of an organization to create increasing value for all of the organization's stakeholders.

The New Era

Each period of business history is characterized by certain conditions or drivers that define the era and result in a set of competitive responses that lead to relative prosperity for businesses who respond effectively. As new drivers emerge, the previous competitive responses become the minimum requirement for entry into the competitive arena or become ballast that must be jettisoned. Experience says that we sometimes have trouble telling the difference.

A brief history of the dominant business eras, with their major drivers and

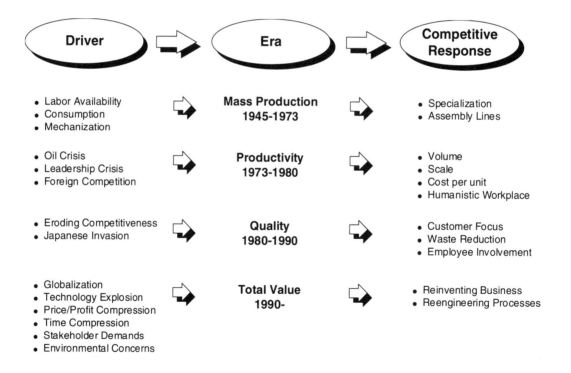

Figure 1.1 Recent Business Eras

competitive responses, is shown in Figure 1.1. The major drivers of the total value era should be described to illustrate how the current era is different from previous periods.

Globalization

With the success of the latest round of worldwide trade agreements and the passage of NAFTA, barriers have begun to come down. The borderless world is becoming a reality that can be dealt with only by what Jack Welch calls the "boundaryless" company. Competitors increasingly see the world as the market. Today's maxim, "If you aren't the best in the world, soon you will face the best as competitors in your market." For example, Goodyear concerns itself with the activities of its chief competitors in Japan and France, not just the tire maker up the road as it did in the past.

Technology Explosion And Information Expansion

CNN and computers mean that worldwide information is available in real time. Real-time information changes everything from business planning to political decision making. Technology reinvents much of our work world as almost every job involves the use of a computer. The microchip has, as Malcolm Forbes Jr. notes, "...extended the reach of the brain much like mechanization extended the reach of muscle at the turn of the century." When everyone in the company can exchange ideas with the CEO via e-mail as Microsoft employees do with Bill Gates, fixed organizational configurations become irrelevant. Computer networks are to decentralization and empowerment what mainframes were to centralization and management by control.

Price/Profit Compression

When the best in the world compete anywhere there is a market, profit margins come from the effectiveness of operations and the quality of the total customer experience rather than from price. Only in economies like Brazil where inflation is catastrophic can one count on riding the tide of ever-increasing prices to higher profit margins. Total value supplied to customers, rather than market-share dominance, creates the ability to establish price leadership. Smaller players providing greater total value can supplant market leaders and win share based on quality *and* price. Domestically, non-value-adding activities such as complex pricing and discounting, including coupons, are being questioned and dropped as consumer goods companies respond to the craving for higher value from customers and consumers.

Time Compression

Speed is one of the drivers of total value. In a real-time world, decision speed must also be made in real-time. Hierarchy and order are not conducive to operating in a fast paced world. *Fleet*, *fast*, *decentralized*, *customized*, and *empowered* are characteristics that replace *hierarchy*, *order*, *controlled*, and *slow*. Customers today expect literally any service or information anytime and anywhere.

Environmental Concerns

The compatible coexistence of business with the environment has become an essential condition of the immediate future. Processes must minimize not only the cost of operation but also the cost to the environment. Costs and effects once hidden are now coming to light as we pay for waste cleanup and struggle to find room for garbage. Collectively, organizations are being made aware that environmentally-unfriendly processes will ultimately have profound negative effects on the sustainability of the planet. The communities in which a company operates are demanding environmental consciousness, community awareness, and support.

Stakeholder Demands

All stakeholders of the organization have raised the ante. Shareowners have urged boards of directors to hold senior managers accountable for performance. IBM, GM, and Kodak fired their CEOs because they were unable to change those massive organizations sufficiently to ensure long-term viability. Total economic return has become the battle cry.

Each of these major forces demands that organizations optimize available resources to create value for all stakeholders. The transition from the customer service and quality era to the era of total value is defined by a new business equation (see Figure 1.2):

Figure 1.2 The Total Value Equation

As with any emerging driver, total value first occurred as a response to increased demands. Those who sought competitive advantage by redefining the business and thus its processes changed the game to that of total value creation. Adopting total value creation as a response to today's drivers forces business process reengineering and organization recreation.

Examples of value creating companies and how they create unique value include the following organizations. Wal-Mart achieved everyday low pricing by reinventing inventory management and supplier partnerships. Compaq Computers redesigned manufacturing and new product development to change the cost/performance ratio of computers. Southwest Airlines cut frills, avoided traditional reservations systems, and used only one kind of aircraft to deliver on its promise of low-priced, impeccable service. Taco Bell turned fast food on its head by creating systems that delivered quality food at value prices. Each company is noted for high quality, great service, and exceptional price. These companies and others paved the way to a new era of competition. They reinvented their businesses and reengineered their processes and people systems to create higher total value for customers.

"Every big company will be a confederation of small ones. All small organizations will be constantly in the process of linking up into big ones."
Robert Reich

In the value era we see certain organizational characteristics emerging:
1. Reconceptualizing products and services
2. Radically redefining business processes
3. Creating synergy between business processes and people systems
4. Redefining customer and supplier relationships
5. Lengthening business horizons
6. Smashing bureaucracy

7. Creating small and fast organizational configurations

8. Extending the web of resources of the company through partnering, outsourcing, and alliances

The Limits Of The Quality Paradigm

In the quality and customer service era, organizations' performance improved largely within an existing set of operating paradigms. The macro design of many work processes remained unchanged and organizational configurations based on functions and hierarchy typically prevailed in spite of the impact of total quality management. Quality improved and waste was reduced, but total value supplied to customers did not necessarily go up. Customers who received better quality and service began to expect those improvements *and* better prices. While arm's-length and even antagonistic relationships between customers and suppliers remained in some cases, leading edge companies began to demand more than just the physical product from suppliers. The quality era established new requirements for total product quality, price, and added services. Wal-Mart, for example, wants suppliers to pass along the benefits of process improvement in the form of better prices, maintain high quality, and cross the customer-supplier boundary to manage price and shelf space for an entire category of products. In short, Wal-Mart requires a total-value supplier.

Staunch advocates of the quality revolution would argue that there is no new era or profoundly new set of methods operating here. Dr. Deming argued that a business has been, and will always be, about optimizing the system of production and service and meeting the spoken and unspoken requirements of

Reengineering Business Processes
and People Systems

its customers. These concepts are unquestionably true, but those conditions have not often been produced by organizations that adopted total quality as a philosophy. Dr. Deming's description of the end-state is profoundly true. The problem is that the mechanisms for creating a system that is continually optimizing its use of resources and anticipating the needs of its customers have been lacking in the implementation of TQM as typically defined.

There is ample research illustrating the limited success of total quality management in America. In one recent survey, ninety percent of CEOs stated that they were unsatisfied with the results of their TQM initiatives. The destination of the quality movement is not in question, but the road home can be too tortuous and slow to traverse. Some of the limits of the quality paradigm as it has been practiced are described below.

Same Target

Focusing on current customer needs and smoother hand-offs across the organization is, in itself, a constrained paradigm. The current customer requirements and organizational boundaries are the constraints. In terms of customer requirements, the issue is whether you are shooting at the right target and using the right projectile. Focusing on the customer was revolutionary for many businesses and an essential first stage, but the focus can become myopic and concretize the current view of the customer, his requirements, and the products and services needed. In the total-value era the price of entry is customer focus, but the steps up the ladder are anticipating new requirements and redefining the products and services to meet current and new requirements. To change the target is to change the business in a fundamental way. Coca-Cola no longer counts on firing its traditional brands at customers when new requirements like healthfulness and variety have emerged in the market. Thus we see the emergence of new products like Fruitopia and PowerAde.

Slow

Quality efforts have often become stalled in their tracks and are slow-moving and unfruitful when fully implemented. There is a faster way to change the current state of an organization and lift it to a new level of play. This comes only by casting out old assumptions about the company, its products, services, and customers and beginning anew with a clean sheet of paper. Plans for rapid change have a greater chance of success. Lawrence Bossidy at AlliedSignal has created a compelling example of rapid change. As an experienced manager of change, Bossidy has been able to bring about a five-year change in less than two years. Pace, permanence, and pervasiveness have been the plague of change efforts. Our efforts aren't fast enough, don't last long enough, and are not all-encompassing enough. New change strategies must conquer these challenges.

Not Potent Enough

Another problem with the quality approach is that its implementation is often not strong enough to break through walls of bureaucracy and move the organization to the next level of competition. There is not enough medicine in continuous improvement to change organizations that were built on a completely different set of principles.

American Philosophy

A final hypothesis that explains the difficulty some have had with total quality is that some of the underpinnings of the quality movement are not fundamentally American enough in nature. It is common to say that Americans have trouble with TQM because they are impatient and want results too soon. One can argue that the notion of incremental improvement is much more an eastern than western one. While continuous improvement has its appeal, the slow process of making gradual change over long periods of time doesn't seem to catch the fancy of Americans. We seem to thrive on tackling something big and producing a result immediately.

"We tend to be good at responding to the wolf at the door, but not the termites in the basement."

David Gergin

In *Incredibly American,* Zuckerman and Hatala offer the hypothesis that Americans are best when there is a crisis. We seem to be at our best when things are at their worst or when we are highly challenged. We seem to need a cliff or a mountain to sustain our motivation. Rather than lament this trait, we should put it to use.

Rather than fight impatience and the desire for results, why not satisfy this urge with a method that requires it as fuel. Reengineering the people systems and processes of an organization is exciting because it promises significant improvements in short periods of time. This formula is much more appealing to the American psyche. Reengineering processes and people systems asks us to reconsider everything and expect dramatic results.

Service Is Not Enough

The quality movement in service industries has focused on providing excellent customer service. This approach often begins at the end of the process, when a problem or complaint occurs, and stays there. We deliver seminars at hotels around the country that are very customer-focused in the sense that employees will readily fix any problem they have created without quibbling. For example, a request for a new arrangement of tables and chairs for the next day is conveyed to your "contact person" who will assure you it will happen. When, as is common, the room doesn't meet your requirements the next day, that same contact person will apologize profusely and have the room changed and deduct any extra charges from your bill. In other words, you can get good service but often not on the first try. In this case, there are no processes to assure that customer changes are incorporated into instructions to the second shift people who will set up the room. The processes haven't changed, and workloads actually increase because problems are always having to be corrected. Prices rise because extra costs are passed on, and overall costs go up. The process-based organization recognizes that a broken performance promise creates cost to the operation, and therefore designs processes that assure complete customer satisfaction on the first go-round.

The Mission Of This Book

The purpose of this book is to help organizations define what the value era means for them and develop new skills, use new tools, and design a change plan to respond to the challenges and opportunities that the future holds. This book is a "how-to" guide for implementing process and organization design. It will go beyond the works that have described the nature and results of reengineering and sociotechnical design and include a methodology and a set of corresponding tools. Some of the areas of emphasis of the book are outlined below.

Don't Obliterate The Human Environment

In his seminal article "Don't Automate, Obliterate," Michael Hammer laid out the essential case for reengineering. He argued for wiping out processes rather than incrementally improving them. Many who follow Hammer's clarion call are wiping out processes and creating much the same effect on the people environment. Much of the heart and soul of organizations are being lost and cannot be regained. Cultures are being destroyed that may never be regained. There seems to be a larger problem dealing with the people who remain in the organization than dealing with those who lose their jobs. To reengineer with the goal of eliminating people is to find an elegant way to shrink, not a way to grow. With this understanding in mind, we will address all aspects of the human environment that will include these topics:

1. Change management — Managing the psychology of change while it is underway
2. People systems design — Defining the optimum environment for people who will operate reengineered processes

Improve The Execution Of Change

In this work, we will couple the concepts of a new era with a more powerful implementation for change methodology. Poor implementation of new ideas has often been as costly as the lack of the new ideas themselves.

We will emphasize several important characteristics of organizational change that are often missing. The first characteristic is the connection of large scale change efforts to organizational planning and strategy. In our experience, many change efforts suffer because their genesis was sparked by a source other than the mainstream organizational planning process. This disconnection at the outset dooms many efforts to the status of "a program." The second emphasis will be on accurately differentiating change strategies and selecting the strategy that meets the need. Many change efforts are adopting the term *reengineering* because as one executive described, "It's the hot new thing, and it's the only way to get budgets to do things." We dilute the potential of our initiatives when we misname them and add to the cynicism of employees who see every intervention as a "flavor of the month" when it doesn't deliver what it promised.

A third area of emphasis is on the effective implementation of plans. For want of some critical ingredient — outrageous objectives, courageous leadership, big-picture perspective, adequate tools, or well-conceived implementation — many efforts fall short of their goal. This book will draw upon our work and research in the broader area of change management. The final section will provide a change management framework that will help assure the effective transition to the envisioned future. Visions turn into mirages when pursued without a plan. We must increase the batting average of efforts in bringing about important change in organizations. The disappointment quotient is: time + money + expectation / results = net satisfaction or disappointment. This quotient has been far too high for our change efforts.

Reengineering is about accelerating the pace of change and putting the leaders of an organization in charge of their fate. It is about engineering not just processes, but the future. Many can articulate reasons for change, but few organizations mobilize the energy of the organization to change in enough time to make a difference.

Napoleon once said, "Armies win wars because they fight other armies." Much the same could be said for why large, slow behemoth-like companies have long lives; it's because they fight other large, slow behemoths. Large organizations unfortunately become unwieldy masses that are much better at maintaining themselves than adapting and adjusting. With size, companies experience an accompanying erosion of the human environment and process capability. Each, unless actively nurtured, tends to maintain itself at best, and more commonly, decay over time.

Changing Large Organizations

Past success has little predictive value identifying which companies will succeed in the 1990s and into the twenty-first century. The venerable companies of the Fortune 500 — GM, IBM, Sears and others — have been exposed as dinosaurs of a previous era. Each is now in the midst of reinvention. New signs of life and innovation, particularly at Sears, offer hope that even these corporate old dogs can learn some new tricks. For other old dogs, not changing creates the need for the draconian measures we see many companies taking. Everyone must change. If you change ahead of the curve, you can capture opportunities and prosper through change. If you are late to respond, you have to take measures that ultimately weaken the company (like cutting 40,000 people). No one views the reductions at IBM as anything other than corrective action for long periods of inaction.

As this new day emerges, companies seek to become the creative, adaptive, and nimble forces that will be required to compete in the turbulent twenty-first century. The new era offers new challenges and new opportunities while old defenses and strategies are rendered useless.

"What we are trying relentlessly to do is get that small-company SOUL—and small-company SPEED— inside our big company body."
Jack Welch

In the value era, companies are breaking up centralized structures and creating constellations of fast, nimble units to serve local markets with customized goods and services. The basis of competition changes as the new form of corporations emerges. The necessity to reinvent, reengineer, and redesign is clear. Size, scale, and capital barriers to entry are tremendous shields that once protected organizations from the outside. These lines of defense are now being made obsolete, much as heavy armor became obsolete for the medieval warrior. As *Fortune's* Thomas A. Stewart notes, "Don't be overly impressed with the height of your walls or the size of your moats; a new competitive era is upon us." It's time to look to the future and recreate the company to match the challenges and opportunities that it will bring.

The basic tenet of this book is that competitiveness derives from the ability of the organization to respond to challenges and opportunities in its environment. Many organizations have lived insulated from changes and challenges and are now feeling the piercing heat as old heat shields are being burned away. In this climate, the ability to anticipate and adapt effectively may be the single most important competitive characteristic. Responding to change in ways that enhance competitiveness separates one competitor from the rest.

Change To Grow And Prosper

Much has been done to reengineer out costs and waste; little has been done to engineer growth. Growth is usually stimulated by much more appealing conditions; opportunity and challenge collide with innovation and invention to provide new opportunities. Cost reduction may be a necessity, but it is most often survival-oriented, rather than prosperity-oriented.

"As in the natural environment of hurricanes and volcanoes, the work environment needs an occasional revolution to generate new life."

Many choose dramatic goals to spur creative thinking in reengineering efforts. These goals should be achievement and advancement rather than retrenchment and defense. Competitiveness is enhanced when great goals to increase market share, grow revenues, and dominate are created. Be careful to set true expansionist goals. Remember that even growing profits can be an illusory measure of long-term success. Simply cut back on investment, over-stretch people for a year, or consolidate operations, and profits will increase. There may be a necessary contraction to prepare for growth, but it is hard to tell this kind of retrenching from a downward spiral of cuts that weaken and lcad to more cuts. Some moves may produce better numbers on Wall Street for a day or a month, but a short-term blip is often a false indicator. What everyone from the shrewd investor to the frontline employee awaits is evidence that the organization is gaining strength and capability.

The hardest, but most powerful thing, an organization can do is set goals that they don't know how to achieve. Great goals are the fuel of innovation and enterprise. Don't let these goals become burdens by telling the world of your great ambitions, but resolve internally to achieve great heights. Leave external expectation management to your spokespeople. Don't confuse managing the psychology of the stock market with internal goal setting. Wall Street expectation setting makes everyone conservative because the stock price is hammered if you miss the goal. The thinking goes, "It's not so much how you do, it's that you accurately predict how good or bad you will do." The boldness required to set goals that you don't know how to accomplish is the creative spark for innovation and the catalyst for motivation.

At the core of the value era is the focus on business from the process perspective. Through the value lens, the processes of an organization are of paramount importance. Great strategy or dynamic marketing amount to little without processes capable of delivering what is promised and what customers want. The process approach asks the business to envision the ideal output (for example, extraordinary service) and then to design processes capable of delivering those requirements.

New Models Around Us

We began addressing the organization as a comprehensive whole under the rubric of sociotechnical design. Beginning with the work of Eric Trist and Albert Cherns at the Tavistock Institute in the 1950s, the idea of sociotechnical design gained a significant following in America in the 1970s. Louis Davis and James Taylor at the University of Southern California's Quality of Worklife Center pioneered many of the revolutionary experiments in the work design of the seventies. The case examples were stunning. A General Foods Gaines pet food plant and a Sherwin-Williams paint plant operated with minimal management and produced the highest quality output. The only complaint about the new approach was that it was difficult to spread because it was so different and threatened the traditional mode of operation.

As reengineering has become popular, our challenge will not be to create excellent models, for many already exist, but to spread the learning and foster rapid change.

2

The Methodology

2

Reengineering Defined

The Methodology

The Methodology

The purpose of this book is to offer the reader a guide book for initiating and conducting a reengineering effort. The methodology begins at the highest level of organizational planning so that decisions to reengineer processes and redesign people systems have a direct link to the vision and strategic direction of the company. Our experience is in the "trenches" of the practical world so we will strive for user-friendly methods and tools. Experience is, however, the best teacher, so we urge you to take what you learn here and begin honing your skills.

This book seeks to be distinctive in four ways:

1. To distinguish between process reengineering and process redesign.
2. To redefine reengineering to include people systems.
3. To offer a method for improving the effectiveness of change initiatives.
4. To offer methods and tools that will make the job easier.

Reengineering Defined

This book by its title intends to provide a methodology for the simultaneous reengineering of selected business processes and essential features of people systems. We will explicitly address the steps necessary to reengineer work processes and concurrently define the desired human environment and culture.

*"The best way
to face the future
is to build it."*

The terminology of this book will be as all-encompassing as possible. We will use the terms *reengineering* and *process redesign* to describe two distinctly different levels of process change. Reengineering a process will mean that the boundaries and outputs of a process will be explored for change. Process redesign will represent less radical change because the existing boundaries and outputs will not be changed, only the work flows and methods inside the current boundaries. We will use the term *people systems* to describe the organizational configuration of an enterprise. People systems will include job design, motivational systems, and management support systems, as well as organization and team structure. It is our view that these areas have received inadequate attention in the reengineering literature. There are many articles and books on contemporary people systems and organizational configurations, but they do not include process reengineering. At the same time, reengineering authors are saying little about people systems and organizational configurations, other than mentioning that they will change dramatically in a reengineered world. The two need to be brought together in the architecture of a reengineered company.

The Methodology

There are six major steps in the process we use in our consulting practice. Each step is briefly outlined in this chapter and elaborated upon in each succeeding chapter. The methodology begins with a reality check of the outside and inside situation. These steps are part of a comprehensive planning process that assures a direct link to the vision and strategic direction of the company.

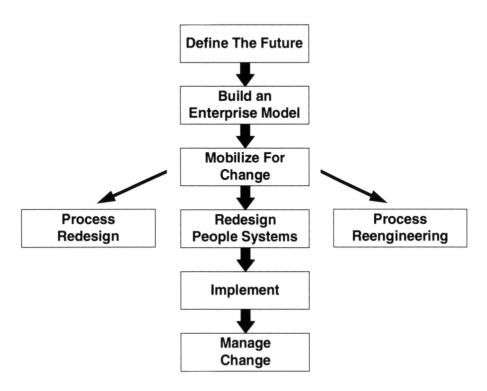

Figure 2.1 Reengineering Methodology

We want to avoid designing a change effort that does not stem from the organization's official priority-setting processes. Even if the user of this book is not in a position to help define the vision and strategy of the company, it is still essential that reengineering and redesign choices be based on them. Reengineering efforts that have a strategic link will be successful; those that don't, aren't worth the time and effort.

Step 1: Define The Future

The steps involved in reengineering the processes and people systems in the organization are depicted in Figure 2.1. The first step in initiating significant organizational change is also a step in the planning process. Planning does not commonly generate change. We know this because strategic planning has been practiced for some time but it has not spawned the kinds of radical changes that we now see as essential in business. Traditional planning had more to do with moving along the same path at an acceptable pace than with dramatically changing paths or speeds. Planning has often been an organizational ritual designed to fix current capability and put a minimum requirement on performance. Planning, as defined here, will be the catalyst for major organizational change and will also assure that the work that ensues will be the real work of the business, not a sideline program. When tough times come, the official objectives get the attention. Fundamental change in the way organizations plan is a key to successful change efforts. In fact, planning should be synonymous with initiating change.

In some cases, the first process to reengineer should be planning itself. To reinvent planning may be to reinvent the business, for the planning period is the one time when the organization looks to the future, takes stock, and mobilizes heart, body, and soul toward important achievements.

Defining the future involves a dynamic interaction of forces, not a linear progression of steps. It is iterative since there is a necessary interplay between three primary sources of input. The first input is the organization's vision, mission, and principles. The second input is an "outside-in" scan, which is based on an assessment of the events and trends in the external environment. The third input is the "inside-out" scan, which assesses the capability of work processes and the current state of the people systems and culture.

These elements are shown in Figure 2.2. Any one without the others is a formula for failure or at least great confusion. The internal elements of the strategic triangle are defined in the sections that follow.

MVP (Mission, Vision, And Principles)

Vision describes the ideal future state of the business. Vision is a picture of the future organization, painted with short, memorable words, that defines a

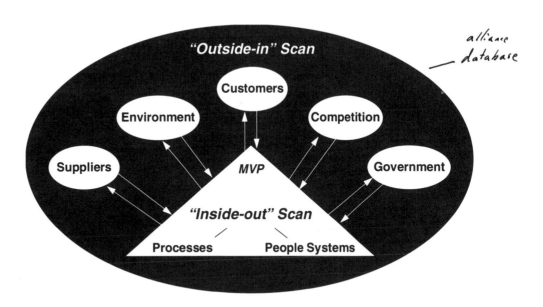

Figure 2.2 Defining the Future: Combining Elements (MVP refers to mission, vision, and principles.)

desired direction and state of being. Vision is the beacon lighting a path toward the future. Ford Motor Company has one of the best and simplest vision statements that says Ford seeks, "...to be the maker of the highest quality cars and trucks in the world." Vision and mission statements are often overworked and hackneyed. They do not represent a source of vital energy, but the fulfillment of a basic requirement of "contemporary" managers. We should use our vision, mission, and principles as drivers of change and set about changing processes and people systems to make the vision possible.

"Inside-out" Scanning Of Processes

Processes are the sets of repeatable activities by which the organization accomplishes its work and produces its goods and services. Process capability is the quantification of the performance of the core processes. It is what you can do day-in and day-out. Much like a runner who trains for a race, organizations develop a certain capability. As with a runner, no amount of motivation can replace the training required to compete at world-class levels when the gun sounds.

Process capability is a strategic asset, sometimes referred to as marketable know-how. It is Wal-Mart's inventory management, Southwest Airline's service, and Chrysler's product development capability. It can be a strategic liability if you need to do things that you cannot do. American automobile manufacturers had to develop the capability to design and produce new automobiles in a three-year cycle rather than the industry norm of five years because competitors with shorter development cycles gained an advantage in responding to the customer. This new capability that Chrysler and Ford have developed is a primary reason that American automakers are competing successfully against Japanese automakers. Process reengineering must improve the capability of the organization's processes on a day-in and day-out basis. Reengineering is about building new process capability and shoring up capability deficits.

"Inside-out" Scanning Of People Systems

People systems create the human environment in which people operate the processes. People systems determine the organization's culture. People systems include: team and job structures, types and levels of management support, information for decision-making and customer feedback loops, performance reviews, formal and informal rewards, compensation, hiring and training, and policies. At present, do the organization's people systems reflect the content of the vision, mission, and principles? Do the people systems support the effective operation of the processes? What change in the external environment or in the processes will necessitate change in the people systems? As an example, imagine that customers indicate that they would like the salespeople in your organization to act more as consultants and problem-solvers rather than simply offering an array of products and services. What people systems would have to be modified to respond genuinely and effectively to that change in the customers' needs? There would be obvious implications for the training, information, and reward systems, and further scanning would probably identify changes needed in other people systems as well.

The "Outside-in" Scan

All planning occurs in a context. Planning must account for factors in the external environment. The reality of the world in which a company operates is the ultimate judge of the effectiveness of any plans. Plans then must be referenced against specific elements in the company's world. Figure 2.2 shows the categories that must be assessed. Each organization must scan the horizon for changes and develop scenarios relevant to that business.

The pace of change is such that, although the length of our foresight hasn't increased, the rate at which dots on the horizon become towering challenges has increased exponentially. What we have to get better at isn't responding to change events once they are apparent, but rather anticipating events with plans designed around several likely scenarios. If you only respond, the pace of change is such that you may not be fast enough to nab an opportunity or to get out of the way of a challenge before it arrives and smashes you. As Rosabeth Moss Kanter has noted, "The mean time between events is often shorter than the mean time between responses." Examples of slow change include IBM staying with mainframes, Sears ignoring Wal-Mart and value pricing, and GM denying the power of its Japanese rivals for too long.

Step 2: Develop An Enterprise Model

Chapter 3 offers an approach for drawing a new picture of the organization that breaks the old paradigms that defined past periods of success. A process view of the business replaces the traditional organization chart. Process maps are becoming at least as common as organization charts in new employee orientations. Tom Peters quotes an executive from 3M who noted, "Competition has changed; now its our flow chart against their flow chart."

The first step toward breaking the functional paralysis that bogs down our organizations today is to see the business from a different point of view. In this section you will draw the enterprise model of your business that distills all of the complexity down to a collection of basic processes. Complexity is what kills many change efforts. We can't make the path simple enough so we lose our way. We often work on broken pieces that, when fixed, don't fit well together. The enterprise model will assure that the change effort is scoped widely enough to assure lasting change.

The enterprise model picture will be the picture of essential simplicity that will be the cornerstone of reengineering. Reengineering is fundamentally about maintaining the simplicity that makes up most businesses. Often we have taken the basics of a business, such as idea generation, manufacturing, selling, and servicing, and made an organization so complex that people who work there have a hard time explaining how things get done. When explaining how work flows through the labyrinth, people often say to us, "It is amazing anything at all is accomplished."

Observers of organizational processes agree that most organizations can be distilled to a few basic end-to-end processes. Thomas A. Stewart contends that the most common processes are production, delivery, and relationship management. Michael Hammer offers product development, sales, ordering, and service as the most common basic processes of a business. The enterprise model defines the core processes that are the heart of the business, the support processes, and the management processes.

The task of labeling these major processes is one of chunking together work that has been previously broken into functions, departments, and sections. For instance, accounting would typically be thought of as different departments

*"This is the
revolution at work:
changing what we do,
how we do it, and
deciding whether
to do it at all."*

or functions that own small pieces of the whole. Groups that handle accounts receivable, accounts payable, billing, and general ledger don't often think of how all the parts comprise a whole process. A new process conceptualization might be the *settlement process* which extends from the point at which goods are ordered until the point that money is in the bank. It might also be called the *order-to-deposit process.*

Step 3: Mobilize For Change

The third step in the reengineering process is to define the scope and reason for mounting a significant change effort. The outputs of the chapter will be to create a manifesto for change which includes the scope of the effort and the compelling case for action. The scope of the effort will be determined by choosing:

- Total reengineering
- Targeted reengineering of selected processes and people systems

After the scope has been defined, a charter is developed, ownership for the change effort is assigned, and a team is put in place to do the reengineering and redesign work. Strategically-driven reengineering is underway at this point and there is no turning back. This step represents the equivalent of Cortez scuttling his ships upon arrival in the new world. He would not be going back without first succeeding.

Step 4: Redesign And Reengineer

The most profound element of reengineering methodology is reconceptualizing the fundamental nature of your work. Chapter 6 addresses the heart of reengineering. This section offers several methods for doing this key task. Figure 2.3 lists the steps in the process reengineering block shown in Figure 2.1. You will adopt a new paradigm for thinking about work and consider fundamental questions about the *why* and *how* of work. To reconceptualize the work we must address these basic questions:

- Can we do without this work altogether?
- Can we combine work across groups that transforms what we do?
- Can we move key aspects of the work upstream to suppliers or downstream to customers to add value and take out cost?
- Can we redefine the boundaries of the process to create ownership of the whole process?
- Can we collapse the time required to perform the work by eliminating everything that does not add value?
- Can we use technology to enable reconceptualized work flows to become a reality?

Chapter 7 is devoted to process improvement. Process redesign is less vast in its objectives and will likely be part of the portfolio of change strategies employed. Process redesign is also a necessary skill for everyone in the organization after reengineering. Process management skills will assure that reengineered processes don't deteriorate to their old state. Some of the limits on process improvement typically are:

- Process boundaries usually don't change.
- Technological changes may be limited.
- Process ownership remains constant.
- Outputs are not redefined.

Process Reengineering

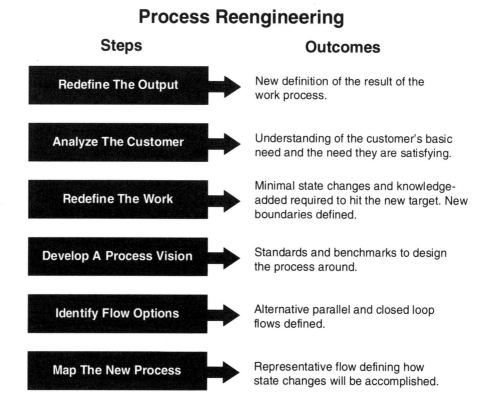

Figure 2.3 Process Reengineering: Specific Steps

Chapter 8 addresses people systems. The elements that define culture must be considered for redesign in parallel with process reengineering. A newly-engineered process will not be successful if people are not organized around it in optimum configuration with the right skills, information, and support to operate it effectively. In this chapter, we will define the organization that lives its principles and jointly optimizes its processes and people environment.

Steps 5 And 6: Implement And Manage Change

While the term *change management* has come into vogue, it most often sounds like telling people what is coming. It is a little like standing on a train track when you hear the whistle blowing. You know it's coming, and all you can do is prepare yourself to get out of the way.

The transition from new process maps and plans for new people systems is a treacherous one. Michael Hammer has been quoted as saying that only about forty percent of reengineering projects are successful. Some of the common causes of failure are:

- Design teams are disbanded after plans are approved, leaving implementation teams disconnected from the original thinking.
- Design teams and leadership teams evolve significantly during their experience and become impatient with the rest of the organization.
- Associates are not left with enough of the details of process operation to figure out on their own and thus reject the new designs out of hand.
- Managers are not trained in a new philosophy of management or do not acquire the corresponding skills.
- The role of internal consultant is not sufficiently fulfilled.
- Leadership does not stick to the change plan.

Chapter 9 will offer a framework for detailing successful implementation plans and defining the essential roles and responsibilities required to bring the paper plans to life in the habits and practices of the people of the organization. Because a book must follow a linear flow, this chapter comes near the end. In reality, the process of managing change begins at the moment you decide to initiate reengineering.

Finally, Chapter 10 offers a variety of reengineering tools, techniques, and training methods.

3

Building A New Organizational Model

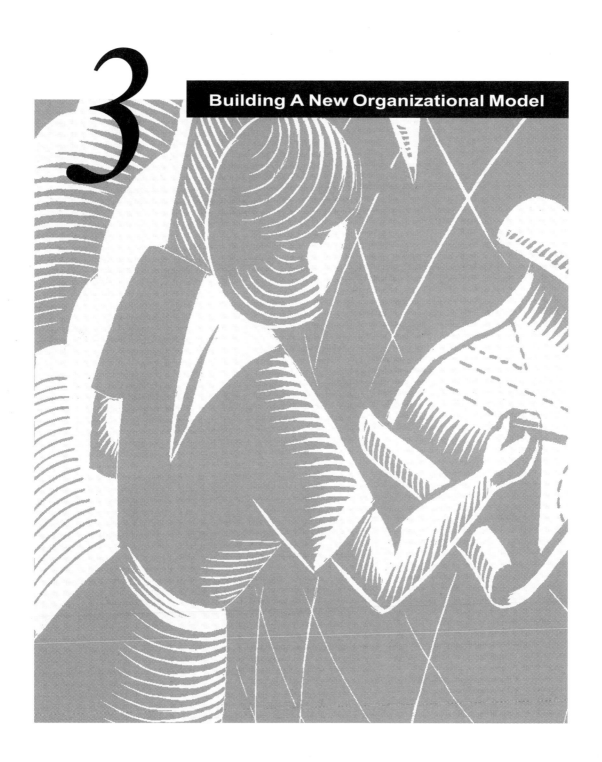

3

Observing The Organization

The Vertical View Of An Organization

The Basics Of Process Thinking

Developing An Enterprise Model

Building A New Organizational Model

There are many lenses through which we can observe an organization from a fresh perspective to spot where value is created and where high leverage improvement opportunities exist. Some of the traditional lenses we use to view an organization are financial measures and performance ratios. What is the company's market position, product line, cost structure, profit margin, stock price, and P/E ratio? Answers to these questions give us some sense of what the organization is all about and its prospects for future prosperity. Other lenses we can use for analysis and greater understanding are constructed of political, cultural, social, technological, and environmental stuff. Each of these perspectives offers a unique view, but may miss what counts most in creating value.

A new lens is being applied to businesses today to discover where the value is created or subtracted. This is the lens of business processes. While the concept of processes has been around seemingly forever, the idea is being applied to organizations in a profound way. The process view has the potential to change how we see the business and how it operates. Because the process view affords a unique look at the whole and a special angle on what the important work of the organization really is, we can get on the fast track for improvement by reinventing how we do what we do. This is the power of the process view that an enterprise model can provide.

Observing The Organization

A grounding in process thinking is the first step in developing this lens. With this foundation, we can reshape the business into a new form that maximizes its capability to create value. But to do this, we have to throw out some old interpretations of the word "process." The word has become synonymous with rules, procedures, and a one-right-way mentality. We know that the government is replete with processes and the amalgamation of these processes has become stifling bureaucracy. The instruction, "Just follow the process," from a governmental agency sounds like, "Wait eternally and follow ridiculous steps."

Even the term "process" itself is sometimes objectionable because of its bad connotations. Some think that focusing on the process means that we are not focusing on the desired result. We believe that this concern is misplaced. In fact, the exclusive focus on results, without an equal focus on processes, is a large part of the reason that processes have become so convoluted that they can't readily accomplish the desired results. So call them workflows, or use any other term, but it's clear that the process view is proving to be the surest way to dramatically improve results. The term process can come to mean the superhighway of work that speedily transforms customer desires into states of satisfaction. In this process world, results aren't less important, rather, it's because the results are so important that we obsess on the processes that produce them.

The Vertical View Of An Organization

A process view is a pure view of what the organization really does. It shows what is done independent of how it is done, who does it, or how people are organized, managed, or staffed. To create a process view, one must recognize that there are two other ways to depict an organization. The first is the traditional organization chart. The chart in Figure 3.1 is much simpler than

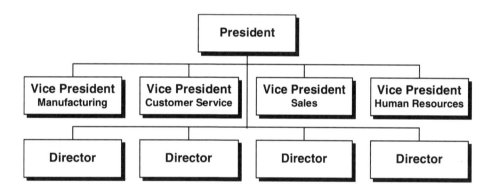

Figure 3.1 The Vertical Organization

most organization charts, which typically take up many pages and are always out-of-date. The most important information conveyed by organization charts is who owns what, and who reports to whom. The vertical view represented in the traditional organization chart influences much of what we see and think about any organization. This vertical view is the organizational chart that anyone working since World War II was raised on. We use it to explain the business. Our vocabulary about work is even sprinkled with vertically- and power-oriented phrases like, "up the ladder," "rise to the top," and "my subordinates." The placement of offices of the highest-ranking executives follows this basic vertical orientation where rank is equated with height.

How we see the organization guides how we manage and operate it. The vertical organization was set up for the management of power and the exercise of control, and it did a very good job of it.

Geary Rummler and Alan P. Brache note:

"...when managers see their organizations vertically and functionally, they tend to manage them vertically and functionally...'Silos' (tall, thick, windowless structures) are built around departments. These silos usually prevent interdepartmental issues from being resolved between peers at low and middle levels...The silo culture forces managers to resolve lower-level issues, taking their time away from higher-priority customer and competitor concerns. Lower-level employees, who could be resolving these issues, take less responsibility for results and perceive themselves as mere implementers and information providers."

Even Rummler and Brache's good advice is spiked with the vocabulary of the hierarchy and verticality they wish to abolish. References to "lower-level issues" and "lower-level employees" connote an almost subliminal view that the issues and people are less important. Illustrating the power of paradigms, it is hard for even the most genuine change agents to avoid the traps of tradition. The organization that seeks breakthrough performance will eliminate the paradigm of superior and inferior people, and important and unimportant problems, and gain its satisfaction from dominating the market rather than its employees. Process thinking is the first big step down this path.

The Functional View

A second way to think about an organization is to understand its functions. The functional organization, born out of the need for order, has obscured our process view. Functionalization followed from our desire for specialization with people doing the one thing they do best. The functional model was to break the processes into pieces for "better management." For example, customer ordering, manufacturing, delivering, and billing are usually managed as functions, each with its own hierarchy and borders. When viewed with the process lens, we see that the functions are actually part of the same larger process. The work can be seen as beginning with an order as the input and ending with money in our bank account as the output. This view leads to different possibilities for effective operation of the process and to different ways to organize people around larger chunks of work.

The organization that has not reengineered is one where the function remains as the organizing model. It made logical sense to put people with similar educational backgrounds together as a function because they did common work. The problem with the model, as we have all experienced, is that the organization of people runs contrary to the way work is accomplished. Design engineers are clustered together into their department, and consumer marketers sit together in their department.

Process thinking helps us make the work we do more basic and more whole. The purpose of a job is much more powerful when it is obviously part of an important whole. So, process thinking is about getting back to the basics of what the business really does and giving people larger shares of the whole.

Clustering people that are alike has been with us since the good readers were called the blue birds and the average readers were the robins. There is an interesting psychological phenomenon that occurs whenever we group people together — groups that are in close proximity and that count on each other soon become competitors and combatants. The links in the process chain that stretch across functions corrode in this functional world. The functional organization is clearly dysfunctional and on its way to the scrap heap. It is being replaced by the process-based organization.

In the process-based organization these former over-the-transom functional duelists are turned into teammates who own a whole process, like the new product development process. The enterprise model will offer this broader view of work, and in so doing, provide insight into who should be organized together based on what is needed to accomplish the work.

The Basics Of Process Thinking

The definition of a process is fundamental to process thinking:

- A process is any repeatable activity or group of activities that takes an input, adds value to it, and provides an output to an internal or external customer.

Process thinking is a basic mental approach that everyone in an organization needs to share in a value-creating company. The process model, at its most basic, is all about value. That model is based on the simple notion that all work begins with input, followed by work activities that produce a transformation of the input into an output. An idea is transformed into a product, a lead becomes a customer, and scrap metal becomes a steel ingot. When a process has operated effectively, the output meets or exceeds the requirements of customers and can be priced to yield a profit. The profit equation, although a very basic idea, often is calculated without real knowledge of the value-adding versus value-subtracting elements of the process. In times past, profit margins could be maintained even if much of the cost of the process was value-

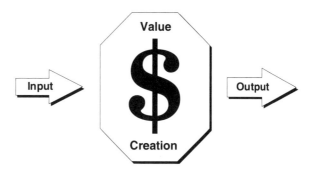

Figure 3.2 The Building Block of Processes: Value Creation

subtracting. With price and profit compression being a reality of our day, one must know where value is created and where cost alone is added. Figure 3.2 depicts this basic concept. The important work is to sort out all the activities occurring inside the box into value-creating and value-subtracting categories. There are no neutral activities; if it doesn't create value it is adding cost.

Identifying Processes

Our daily work is nothing but process. However, a process view is often obscured by other potent organizational aspects. Tasks, job assignments, reporting relationships, pay systems, and political issues are often more salient organizational elements that command our attention. But work, whether accomplished through super-highway-like processes or through processes that are more like an English garden maze, is done via a process. Historically, we made work more manageable by breaking it into smaller and smaller pieces. What often resulted was a work arrangement in which we lost all sight of the larger process. The idea of a larger view is central to this chapter. Process improvement has been a part of the total quality world since its inception, but unfortunately much of this improvement work occurred within narrow process boundaries. The enterprise model will offer the widest possible view of the organization's processes, and in so doing allow us to not only improve, but to reinvent the processes.

A possible source of trouble in thinking of our work as a process may occur when work produces intangible products, like recommendations or sales presentations. In these knowledge-work processes, the repeatable workflows are not as obvious as they are in manufacturing, and people are the most obvious improvement levers. When something goes wrong, the analysis lens that is often used is the one that focuses on the motivation and skill of people. Broken processes that frustrate associates and managers can go unexamined for years until we put on our process glasses.

Going beyond a definition of work as tasks and activities to a definition of work as a series of processes is an important first step in re-framing work. All work can be thought of as a process when we view it as a repeatable sequence beginning with input and transforming that input into valuable output. The second major step will be to broaden the definition of the processes themselves so that they become the end-to-end workflows rather than walled-off independent work centers. Process thinking is characterized by:

- Defining work as a process, with inputs from suppliers and outputs to customers.
- Understanding how the process really works.
- Focusing on improving process construction before people performance.
- Thinking of managing processes not functions.
- Thinking end-to-end from the customer perspective.

Types Of Organizational Processes

The final output of this chapter will be to develop an enterprise model of your organization. In order to do this, we first begin with a basic definition of the types of processes that are typical in an organization.

Core Organizational Processes

Core organizational processes are the large-scale, fundamental processes that represent the mission of the organization. Core organizational processes, such as new product development or order delivery, hold the greatest opportunity for performance improvement for two reasons. First, virtually every team and individual can influence these processes in either a positive or negative way. Second, since a key organizational process often does not fall neatly within the boundaries of a single function, it often goes unstudied in its entirety.

Third, because organizational barriers often exist among different functions, the workings of a key organizational process can become very convoluted. Examples of core organizational processes are the consumer marketing process at Proctor & Gamble, the inventory management process at Wal-Mart, and the new product development process at 3M.

Standard Processes

Standard processes are processes that everyone in an organization should do the same way. Process improvement plans for such processes can be disseminated throughout an organization to minimize unnecessary variation and "reinventing the wheel." Standard processes can include administrative processes such as ordering and invoicing, and common work processes such as planning, budgeting, and project management.

The opportunity to examine and improve processes that operate everyday throughout an organization is enormous. In some organizations there can be literally dozens of ways of managing projects, doing budgets, and writing reports. The need for standardization and consistency is clear.

New Processes

New processes are processes being started from scratch as a result of a new product, customer, or technology. A new process offers the chance to engineer the workflow according to contemporary thinking so that it won't need to be reengineered in the years ahead. The construction of new processes will likely become necessary as the enterprise model is evolved. Many organizations discover when they build the ideal enterprise model that there are processes that should be operating that are not. The need for a process like, "staying ahead of customers" may be identified during this exercise.

Support Processes

Support processes include the activities that are necessary for operating the core processes. These processes may provide financial analysis, legal recommendations, or information services that the core process cannot produce itself. Support processes of the future may be databases and expert systems rather than functions. Today many in staff support positions serve as the human interface between the core process and the database or stored expertise.

Management Processes

Management processes represent the workflows that produce the organization's mission, vision and strategy. These processes assure that the organization maintains permeable boundaries to its environment and corrects its course when necessary. Developing organizational architecture and infrastructure and building organizational capability should also be included within the family of management processes.

Developing An Enterprise Model

An enterprise or process model of an organization is the highest-level view of how the organization accomplishes work. There are several ways to depict the organization as an enterprise. There seems to be as much personality to these models as there are organizations that are developing them. The primary purpose is to show the core processes and create a new basis for

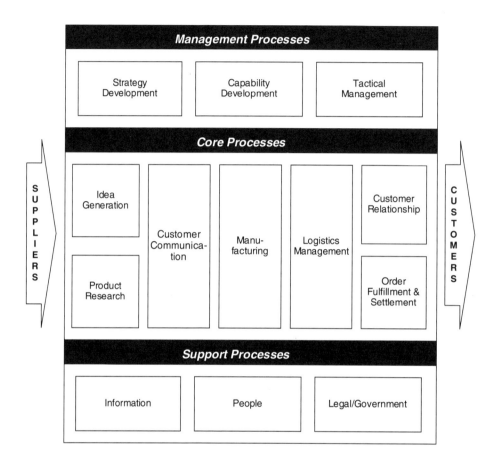

Figure 3.3 An Enterprise Model

organizing and accomplishing work. The diagram in Figure 3.3 is an example of
one organization's enterprise model. The model represents the organization as
a collection of processes that offers an entirely new look at how the important
work is accomplished.

The creation of an enterprise model is an iterative process. The final product is something of a work of art when it is drawn. The important criterion is to show how the processes interact and depend on each other. After all, it is a conceptual model not a Polaroid picture. The model should be technically correct in that the core organizational processes are completely defined. The processes in the enterprise model should be:

- Defined with boundaries that stretch laterally across functions.
- As all-encompassing of related activities as possible.
- Based on outputs that are important to customers.

Steady State And Future State

There are two kinds of enterprise models. The first are steady-state pictures of the organization as it operates today, and the second type are more radical reconceptualizations of the processes of the business. This latter model shows how the work might be redefined, while the former model provides a necessary first step away from the vertical and functional views.

A steady-state enterprise model shows the flow of work between the organizations current work units. It is a high level view of how work flows based on how the organization is configured. It is a first step in building an enterprise model. A steady-state model should illustrate:

- How work flows across the organization today.
- Key hand-offs and interdependencies.

The steady-state model will not follow the organization chart. Power and authority relationships between people will not be depicted. A steady-state model should help the organization look at itself differently as a horizontal flow of work, perhaps for the first time.

Figure 3.4 offers an example of a steady-state enterprise model. This

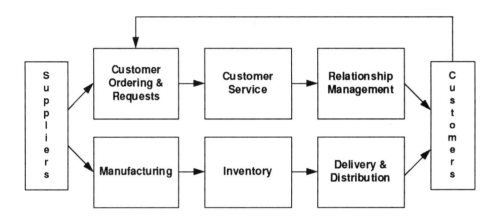

Figure 3.4 A Steady-State Functional Enterprise Model

model shows work flowing between functions or organizational units. The functions haven't changed, but in this simple rendition of a process model, the horizontal flow of work and the interdependencies among groups is illustrated. The organization is shown as a flow of inputs that moves through functions and arrives at customers. The picture is very different from the traditional organization chart and offers a start at redefining the business.

From Function To Pure Process

The next evolution of the model after developing the steady-state picture is to search for the end-to-end processes. The simplest way to define broad processes is to begin with the key organizational outputs. In the model below, we may define the key outputs as "delivered products" and "serviced equip-

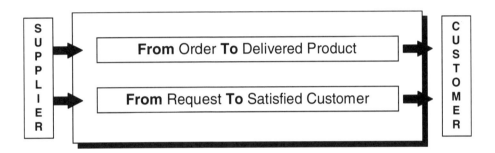

Figure 3.5 A Core Process Model

ment." With these two outputs defined, we should go back to the beginning of the model and ask where the work begins that produces these outputs. To define the work this way, it is helpful to adopt the basic process definition format of From <u>Input</u>/To <u>Output</u>. Filling in the blanks offers the first broad-based definition of the core processes that cut across the functions. In our example, the processes are: From Customer Order To Delivered Product and From Customer Problem To Resolved Problem. Figure 3.5 shows how we could begin to construct our new enterprise model based on this process definition.

The totality of work can be captured in the two major processes that take orders and turn them into delivered goods and take requests and turn them into satisfied customers. With this view, we are free at last from the constraints of how we have organized people into boxes and how we have chunked work into functions. Now we can really think about what is essential to accomplish the From/To transformation.

This is the essential work involved in developing a process model: to draw a picture of the organization that shows the most basic view of what the work is. We have been so trapped by our definition of who does it and how work is accomplished that we are often unable to see another way. The pure end-to-end process view sets us on a path of breakthrough thinking.

Other examples of the From/To construction being used to define broad processes are included here. These three core processes may represent the whole business of an organization. Try to do the same for your organization:

- **From** idea **to** new product design
- **From** raw material **to** finished goods
- **From** customer order **to** cash

It is commonly held that organizations that look at their business in this way will define a handful of processes. In the generic process organization you may have processes such as these described by Ostroff and Smith in *Fortune:*

- Order generation and fulfillment
- Integrated logistics
- Commercialization of technology

Steps For Defining An Enterprise Model

Although it is an iterative process, it helps to follow a logical sequence as you develop your enterprise model.

1. Develop a functional enterprise model of your business (see Figure 3.4).

2. Define the products and services of the company.

3. For each of the key company outputs (products and services), brainstorm as many all-encompassing definitions following the From/To format as possible.

4. Have team members draw a picture that illustrates the processes and shows their interactions.

5. Test interdependent processes to assure that input requirements are matched with an output.

If this approach is not fruitful, or if you are concerned that drawing the functional model will cement its validity, another approach is available. In this method, we take advantage of the fact that it is easier to talk about what we do than it is to think of processes or to talk about why we do it. We work from an anchor of familiarity, our work activities, to define the core processes of the business.

The activity method begins with the basic question, "What do we do here." With answers to this question, list the major categories of work activity in your organization. Then, on either side of the activities make room for two columns. In the left column, write "Because," and in the right column, write "So That." Figure 3.6 shows this construction. This worksheet helps identify the work of the organization and why it is done. The "So That" column offers

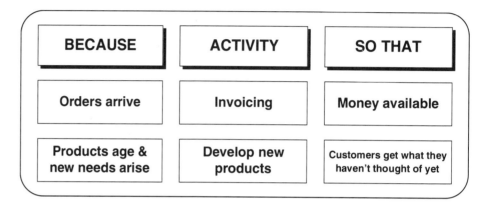

Figure 3.6 An Activity Diagram

reasons for the work and is a clue about what the essential process output is. The activities themselves are only important because of what causes them to be necessary and what effects they produce. The "Because" answers offer a starting point for process definition. The steps in this method are as follows.

1. Brainstorm all of the major activities that are performed in the organization, and combine them into categories.

2. Use a format like the one in Figure 3.6 to analyze the activities.

3. The "So That" column defines outputs or desired conditions the activity is designed to produce. This begins to explain the "Why" of the activity in terms of the output it produces.

4. Next, fill in the "Because" column. This defines the initiator or starting point of work activities.

5. The "Because" and "So That" columns offer a starting point for defining From/To process definitions.

6. Attempt to combine rows into broader process definitions.
7. Draw the processes into a visual picture showing their relationships.

The end result of the enterprise modeling session should be a few core processes. Support and management processes can be conceptualized in the same From/To construction. Any process definition should be challenged to extend its boundaries. Wherever you start, think of adding the adjacent activities and see if a more complete process picture emerges.

The result should be a handful of macro processes. One organization we are familiar with defined eight macro processes and then decomposed these eight into 60 subprocesses. You may begin to improve any one of the subprocesses with the broader knowledge of the whole system and how the pieces fit together. This will allow you to avoid "suboptimization," that is, the radical improvement of one piece of the system that in turn hurts the total system.

It is important to begin process reengineering at the level of the enterprise model. From this level, you can begin "peeling the onion" and focusing on specific processes. It is dangerous to go the other way and say, "Let's start with something we know doesn't work very well, like the billing process, and go from there." Limited benefits come from projects that are scoped within the existing definitions of processes. We have to tackle process definitions that cut across boundaries to make a difference worth the effort.

A narrowly defined process will be hard to change substantially because its reason for being is based on where it fits in a larger process picture. It can be a little like redesigning the bathroom of a house without changing the layout of the adjoining rooms. It can be a better bathroom, but there is a limit to the benefits gained. Rather, begin at the enterprise level with strategically-significant processes and change those with the highest leverage for producing improved business results. As with the house, redesign the whole process for maximum impact.

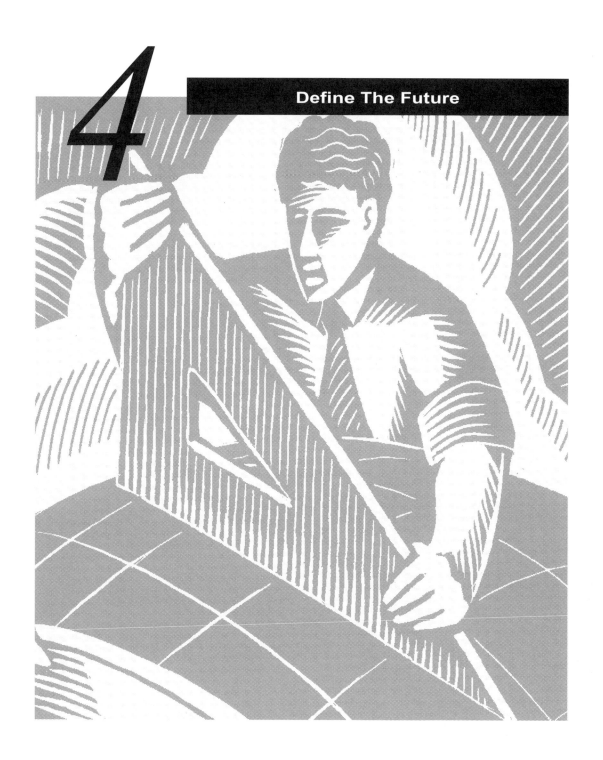

4

Define The Future

4

Paradigms Past

Define The Future As Impetus For Change

Creating An MVP Organization

Scanning

    "Inside-Out"

    "Outside-In"

Define The Future

Process-oriented and value-based organizations are shattering the horizontal boundaries that have hobbled the effective flow of work within and among companies. Horizontal company boundaries are stretching up the chain to the supplier of the raw materials and down the chain through the distributors and retailers to the consumer. Virtually all of the boundaries of business are being redrawn. The supplier is managing the category of products at the retail level, and "looking into" the customer's computer system to keep inventory at optimum levels.

"The beginning is the most important part of the work."

Plato

This reframing of work boundaries is being driven by the broadest extension of process thinking. An organization can see its processes as a complete loop where all of its outputs eventually affect, or even become, input back into the system.

To operate the horizontal value-creating organization requires completely different management "software." This new software will be based on new paradigms or lenses through which we observe and design our organizations. Past paradigms of management will keep the new organization from emerging. It pays to understand our roots before defining the future. Those who know their history won't be doomed to repeat it.

Paradigms Past

Charlie Chaplin's *Modern Times* offers an excellent illustration of old models of work and management. The movie shows a system that has long since outlived its usefulness although vestiges of it live on today. In the first five minutes of the film, Chaplin depicts the life of employees on an assembly line in the 1930s. From the day's beginning, where a faceless mass arrives like a herd of sheep, until the final whistle that signals the end of the day, the employee is at the mercy of a system that manages and controls his every move.

The worklife of the time offered little in the way of dignity or self control. In this all-too-realistic parody, the president is seen as a "big brother" who watches the production process from a wall-sized monitor and regularly sends orders on the intercom for the foreman to "speed 'er up." The president ponders over a jigsaw puzzle between sharp glances at the screen to monitor the working masses.

"Clearly the most unfortunate people are those who must do the same thing over and over again, every minute, or perhaps twenty to a minute. They deserve the shortest hours and the highest pay."
John Kenneth Galbraith

Workers are shown as independent and replaceable parts that only relate to each other when the upstream worker causes a problem for the downstream worker and a fight ensues. Each worker is a solitary performer eking out a living and surviving an oppressive system. Chaplin plays a "bolt tightener" on an assembly line comprised of other equally menial jobs. Man as machine was the model of the day and Chaplin shows its exquisite pain.

Chaplin's comedy is entertaining and poignant in a scene in which he finally takes his allotted break from the mind-numbing drudgery of the line. After punching his time card he walks to the bathroom, still twitching as he walks in the rhythm of bolt tightening. The staccato music turns to soft mellifluous tones as he finds his only solace in the peacefulness of the bathroom and prepares to light a cigarette. The cherished moment of relaxation is broken as the president appears on the big screen in the bathroom and barks, "Hey you, get back to work. Go on, stop loafing." Back to the enervating monotony of the job he goes, kicked out of the one place where he could make a decision.

The fundamental principles of control management, task specialization, and man as machine are played out. The film is instructive because our perspective as observers lets us see how foolish the whole arrangement is. Narrow jobs, internal focus, and parent-child relationships obviously limit the whole system. Unfortunately, if we become objective observers of the movies being played out in our own workplaces today we would find plenty of subject matter for a similar parody.

Chaplin's classic film mocks the world view of the day. If genius is the ability to have perspective during one's own time, then Chaplin shows his genius. The paradigms of the day — workers are lazy, managers are in a different class, work should be made mindless — were the accepted reality and even viewed as the essentials of industrial prosperity. Despite its great success in these early days, the typical assembly line design was seen by Chaplin as a system that optimized production at the expense of the worker and even at the expense of the customer.

Shedding The Shackles Of The Past

The residue of these paradigms of past success is hard to leave behind as we face the future. We seem always to cling to the past as we are thrust unwillingly toward a changing future. Paradigms are like glue: they stick us to a point in time and a set of circumstances in which they were justified. Then circumstances change and we can't change our paradigms. We are stuck.

Paradigms aren't easily recognizable because they represent deeply held beliefs. We often urge companies to revitalize long-standing values and principles but to lose old paradigms. Principles, such as trust, tend to wither under the stress of high demand, while old paradigms, such as high control, flourish. Paradigms are hard to break because they are the thought models that have helped us succeed. As Napoleon said to Robert Fulton when presented with the idea of a steam-powered ship, "What, sir, you would make a ship sail against the wind and currents by lighting a bonfire under her decks? I pray you excuse me. I have no time to listen to such nonsense."

"In the era of mass production, we made things and let people buy them. There was very little competition."

Whether you trace the business management model of the 20th century to economist Adam Smith, industrialist Henry Ford or efficiency expert Frederick Taylor, the remnants of the paradigms of the past are everywhere. Michael Hammer argues that the job segmentation that characterized this era required layers of management to put the parts back together. He describes the phenomenon as "the Humpty-Dumpty effect." Only at the highest level did anyone see how all the pieces come together to form the whole. Low-intelligence job design and fragmentation of the work require lots of glue to hold it all together. The more we break work apart, the more resources are required to knit it all back together.

The eras of mass production and productivity were characterized by a high command-and-control mentality. These historical periods were dominated by American icons like Henry Ford and George Patton. High control was fine in Ford's day when workers spoke different languages and education was low. Command worked well for Patton — he was commanding 19-year-old men with six weeks of training — but not now when 19-year veterans know more about the work than their manager does. These management paradigms have become outdated today when workers have education and experience.

To break into the new era of value creation we can't afford to operate our organizations on seventy-five-year-old assumptions. It is as though we bought a new Pentium-based computer and loaded it with outdated mainframe software. We are challenged to examine the basic principles and assumptions that built our businesses and to be prepared to cast them aside as we plan the future. Defining the future is the first major step in reengineering and should drive change by embracing new paradigms. This step will help the organization get in touch with two realities: the new demands of the external world and the magnitude of change required.

Defining The Future As The Impetus For Change

Unfortunately, plans for change arc often hatched independent of the formal planning process of the organization. They arise out of needs and situations that are identified during the year. Because of this separation at birth, change efforts often have a hard time being strategically relevant and real to associates who already have a full plate. It makes no sense to devote effort to improve processes that are not central to the success of the business.

The Inputs To Defining The Future

Figure 4.1 shows the key inputs to defining the future. These three inputs are essential to planning for fundamental change. The first input is the organization's constitution — its vision, mission, and guiding principles. The second source of input comes from an "outside-in" scan of the external environment to identify challenges and opportunities. The third input comes from an "inside-out" scan of process capability and organization culture. These three sources of input assure that the organization's change effort will zero in on the right processes and people systems.

Plan For Great Achievements

A change effort must be a central feature of any plan about the future of the business to be successful. If a change effort isn't about shaping the future described by the plans, it is not a real change effort. And if planning isn't about reaching a desirable vision and mission, it doesn't produce much of a plan.

Change initiatives should create the straightest line between the present and the organization's vision and mission. One reason that some doubt the value of vision statements as an impetus for change (for example, Louis Gerstner's early no-vision pronouncements upon becoming chairman of IBM) is that they are not often accompanied by change initiatives that are designed

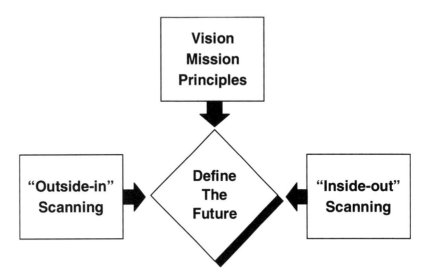

Figure 4.1 Inputs to Defining the Future

to reach the destination. A well done planning process systematically aligns the organization around a common vision, mission, and path and defines the change initiatives required to reach that future.

Traditional plans maintain the status quo rather than serve as a catalyst for change. Planning can become just a budgeting and accounting process. It can be an arithmetic exercise of disaggregating not-so-lofty performance goals from the top. A habit of many organizations is to develop achievable plans, not plans that meet and exceed customer requirements and create competitive advantage. Our reward systems often favor a team that hits a low target and punishes a team that misses a high target. This institutionalizes the acceptance of mediocre performance. In contrast, Engelhard Corporation initiated a reengineering effort with what they called an *outrageous objective* — to reduce manufacturing costs by 20% in twelve months. Since the objective seemed impossible, consideration of radical change was assured.

Business success today is more dependent on how well plans and strategies are executed than on the overall brilliance of the strategy. We hear customers cry, be strategic but give us cars that don't break down, tools that do their jobs, and service that delights. As a wise man once said, "All great strategy eventually deteriorates into work." How well the work is done is where the rubber meets the road. A fair strategy executed to perfection is far superior to a great strategy executed poorly.

Creating An MVP (Mission-Vision-Principles) Organization

In the final scene of the 1954 movie *Executive Suite,* William Holden captures the essence of vision, mission, and principles. Holden plays McDonald Worling who speaks to the board of directors about what it will take to resurrect the suffering but once proud Treadway Furniture Company. The meeting is held to elect a new president to replace the founder who has died. Holden and the rest of the board listen patiently as the company's financial officer argues his case to become president. He claims that dividend growth has been exceptional and that the company would do even better if he can become president and pursue a rational financial path. Holden rises and begins his soliloquy. He asks the financial officer if dividends are everything, "...if your life success will be marked with the dividend record of the Treadway Corporation on your tombstone?"

Worling continues speaking as he strides to one of the new end-tables the company has started to make. He reaches down and rips off one of the legs of the low-quality table and challenges the group, "Is *this* what Treadway has come to mean, what customers can expect? Legs that will fall off and veneer that cracks?" "That's price merchandise," retorts the CFO, "eventually we can make less of it." "We'll drop that line," fires Holden "and we'll never again ask a man to do work that poisons his pride in his work or himself." In full gear, Holden continues, "We are going to make furniture that has beauty and function and value, and we're going to do it together. We're not going to die, we're going to live and it's going to take the strength and ingenuity of every man and woman in this company." On the strength of the picture he presents, painted with words of vision, mission and principles, McDonald Worling is unanimously voted as the new president of Treadway.

Every person who has ever seen this clip has been moved by the power of the message. It is no Pollyanna message. It has a hard-nosed business tone that defines success in terms of the kind of company people want to be a part of and the level of achievement (in financial, customer, and employee terms) that it will take to become that company. Holden's character talks about what the company can be, what it has to do, and what it will believe — the framework we have come to call the organization's constitution, its vision, mission, and principles.

After showing this clip to a senior team, one of the team members, strongly moved by the message, urged his teammates, "That's what we need to hear, that's what our associates need to hear, we don't talk like that around here. We don't speak from the heart, we speak from the spreadsheet." The

"Vision is the art

of seeing things

invisible."

Jonathan Swift

words of the organization's constitution must be a rallying cry and must create
significant dissonance. If upon reading a company's constitution people don't
say, "Boy, that sure isn't us," there probably is not enough stretch in the words.
It takes real leadership and courage to write what is not yet true and rally
everyone around the task of making the words come true.

Vision

Vision is not about the words, it's about the feeling and clarity of the
picture that the impassioned words create. Envisioning the future is the most
important spark in the process of defining change. The vision is the "why" of
change. Visioning is quite different from predicting the future. Prediction is
nearly impossible as evidenced every year by those who try to predict the
stock market or the Super Bowl (even though there seems to be a relationship
between the outcomes of the two).

He who would predict the future is limited by what can be seen. The
ancient Greeks reminded themselves of this limitation by describing a man
attempting to predict the future sitting with his back to the future as today's
events zoom by his peripheral vision and the past is seen with 20-20 clarity.
The advantage those who envision the future have over the man sitting back-
wards is that the visionary can make the future come true. He or she can
"will" the future to happen if enough people share the vision.

 • **Vision:** What we would like to *be* in the future.

Define Your Vision

Imagine that a reporter from *The Wall Street Journal* is writing a story

"A vision is a target

that beckons."

Warren Bennis

about your company five years from now. Write the lead paragraph for the article that will capture the reader's attention about the special things that have taken place at your company. Have each member of the team read his or her paragraph. Write on flipcharts the major themes that are represented in each contribution. Begin to craft a vision statement with these ideas as a core.

Mission

The mission statement describes the accomplishments that will move the organization toward the vision. The mission statement should answer the questions, "What are we in business to accomplish?" and "What specific accomplishments will pave the path toward our vision?"

- **Mission:** What will we have to *do* to reach our vision.

Defining the desired level of achievement in categories of performance begins to define the mission. Common categories include:

- Market performance
- Product performance
- Process performance
- Organization culture

Define specific measurable levels of achievement in each of the mission categories. These mission elements should define three- to five-year accomplishments that can be measured. Developing a complementary set of mission measures to track progress against the mission is essential to keep the words based on reality.

Principles

Principles are the foundation of common beliefs that guide the decisions and choices on the road toward the vision. Principles help define the architecture of a company that will be able to reach the vision, execute the strategy, and inspire the best performance in people. Principles should reflect the new paradigms that the organization chooses to adopt.

"Dare to be naive."

R. Buckminster Fuller

- **Principles:** What we believe to be universal truths about the workplace that are best for people and serves as a basis for the construction and operation of our business.

Principles can be developed by answering the following questions.

1. What assumptions do we choose to make about the nature of people?

Answers could include:

- People are honest.
- People want to do challenging and enjoyable work.
- People can be trusted.

2. What new paradigms do we want to state about workplace design?

Answers could include:

- Work processes should add value at every step.
- Horizontal boundaries should be minimal and permeable.
- Managers are here to support and coach people to improve our processes.

GE chairman Jack Welch's principles are relevant here.

- Face reality as it is, not as it was or as you wish it were.
- Be candid with everyone.
- Don't manage, lead.
- Change before you have to.
- If you don't have a competitive advantage, don't compete.
- Control your own destiny, or someone else will.

With a vision, mission, and principles, an organization can take the second step in defining the future. Scanning allows the organization to match organizational *capability* with external *opportunities* to move the organization toward its vision. Scanning is a way of looking outside and inside the organization to determine what and how much to change.

Scanning

Scanning has two components: the "outside-in" scan and the "inside-out" scan. Outside-in scanning surveys the environment and analyzes trends. Inside-out scanning surveys scanning processes and core people systems. The results of scanning, coupled with the vision, mission, and principles, provide a high-level view of opportunities, challenges, and capability gaps. The following sections of this chapter are on scanning and will complete the process of defining the future.

The "Outside-in" Scan

Reality is one of the straightest doses of medicine one can take — and one of the surest sources of energy for change. Many times seminar attendees say, "It would be great if our organization had a really compelling reason to change, like if we were going out of business." Like the old Hungarian proverb says, "Be careful what you wish for." If the situation today is already urgent, then the company has at best a 50-50 chance of surviving and prospering after the crisis. Every organization has a crisis, if it stays the same long enough into the future. The key to outside-in analysis is to bring the events of the future into today's reality. This process can create urgency in even the most comfortable situations because of the rapid rate of change in our world today. What company can say that it can stay the same for the next five years and still thrive?

The current situation must be fully understood in terms of future opportunities and challenges. We often fail to capture the essence of the situations in which we find ourselves. The outside-in analysis looks for events and trends that challenge the organization to improve or build process capability, as well as those that represent opportunities that can be captured with current capability.

The worksheet in Figure 4.2 offers a simple method for cataloging the trends and factors that we observe. When they are listed together, we see new patterns and trends that define opportunity. Ignoring emerging trends is the fastest way to go out of business. For example, IBM continued to see the mainframe as the core of their business in spite of enormous data that said that PCs and networks held the largest growth opportunities.

	Observation	Opportunity	Challenge
Markets			
Customers			
Technology			
Social			
Government			
Trends			

Figure 4.2 A Worksheet for the "Outside-in" Scan

The "Inside-Out" Scan

The next step in defining the future is to honestly and fairly assess the capability of the organization's processes. This capability analysis begins with the identification of the core business processes and a quantification of the performance capability of those processes.

To do this effectively, it is important to have a macro view of the organization as a series of primary work processes. The enterprise model from the previous chapter fulfills this requirement. Most organizations can be conceptualized as a handful of processes. Some of the common processes are listed below. The completed enterprise model will provide the high-level process

Process:_____

_____

	Current Strengths	Current Gaps	New Requirements
Cost			
Quality			
Speed			
Customer Satisfaction			

Figure 4.3 A Worksheet for an "Inside-out" Scan

definition required for this process capability scan. Common processes are:

- Customer ordering
- Delivery
- Product service
- Customer service
- Manufacturing

Scanning Processes

A total value mindset asks us to evaluate our processes in four categories: *cost, quality, speed* and *customer satisfaction.* Each category may suggest a weakness to shore up or an improvement that would provide a strategic advantage. Questions include:

- Where would improvement in cost, quality, speed or customer satisfaction provide the greatest competitive advantage for our company?
- How can we leverage what we do well to satisfy the requirements of our customers and capitalize upon the opportunities in the marketplace?
- What gaps exist between what we are promising our customers today and our actual performance?
- Which gaps must be closed to avoid erosion of our customer base?
- What new requirements must we meet to satisfy emerging needs?
- What new processes must we design to be able to develop new products and satisfy unstated future needs of our current and future customers?
- What are we unable to do today, that if we could, would give us a great advantage over our competition?

Based on the answers to these questions, complete the worksheet in Figure 4.3. As a result of this analysis you can prioritize the need for process capability initiatives.

Scanning People Systems

The final step in defining the future is to scan all of the people systems and compare them against the organization's constitution and the internal

capability required to operate and develop core processes. People systems
include:

- Team and job structures
- Types and levels of management support
- Information and feedback systems
- Reward and evaluation systems
- Hiring, training, policies, and symbols

The configuration of people systems almost always lags far behind the
evolution of technology or even process construction. Bureaucracy has grown
into the organization like weeds weakening an old sidewalk. Silo walls have
grown stronger as fiefdoms have been built and nurtured.

The configuration of the organization and its very culture must be part of
the thinking as change initiatives are planned. During this scan, pay close
attention to the principles and paradigms defined in your constitution. For
example, a new principle may say, "Management should only add value that
customers are willing to pay for." As you scan the people systems, you would
look for structures, roles, and policies that contradict this principle. Based on
this principle, you may conclude that the number of levels of management
hinders the organization's ability to operate processes and develop people. A
picture of a self-managed organization may begin to emerge during the scan.
The principles should force debate and distinct choices about the blueprint for
the organization. Chapter 8 guides a design team through a more thorough
examination and redesign of people systems once the scan has identified key
areas for change. To identify key people systems for redesign, the following

questions should stimulate useful discussion. The outcome will be a decision to pinpoint specific people systems for improvement or to include all people systems as part of a total reengineering effort. The questions that stimulate this discussion include the following:

1. What characteristics must be common in our culture if we are to live our principles and reach our vision?

2. Where are the most significant gaps between how we operate today and how we would operate if our principles were fully operational?

3. What barriers in our structure make it hard to accomplish work?

4. Where have we broken whole processes into specialized pieces unnecessarily?

5. What is the current role of managers and what should it be?

6. What is the current ratio of managers to associates and what should it be?

7. Which jobs in our organization are so narrow that they inhibit personal growth and whole-process operation?

8. How do our evaluation and reward systems match or conflict with our newly-defined principles?

9. Where could information systems be improved so that associate-level teams could make important process decisions?

10. How could we improve the way all of the organization's members stay current with performance and receive regular feedback from customers?

11. Do we have unnecessary policies and rules?

12. How do associates become oriented to our company's constitution and use it to define their own unique contribution as part of a team?

13. How could we improve how associates are trained?

14. What skills will be required in the future that we are not proficient at today?

Defining The Future Produces Strategic Choices

The outputs of defining the future — vision, mission, and principles, the "outside-in" scan, and the "inside-out" scan of processes and people systems — produce strategic choices. Strategic choices are the opportunities, challenges and gaps that the change effort will address (see Figure 4.4).

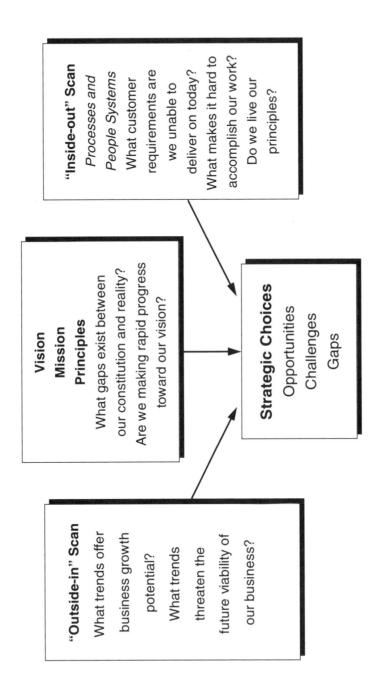

Figure 4.4 Achieving Strategic Choices

5

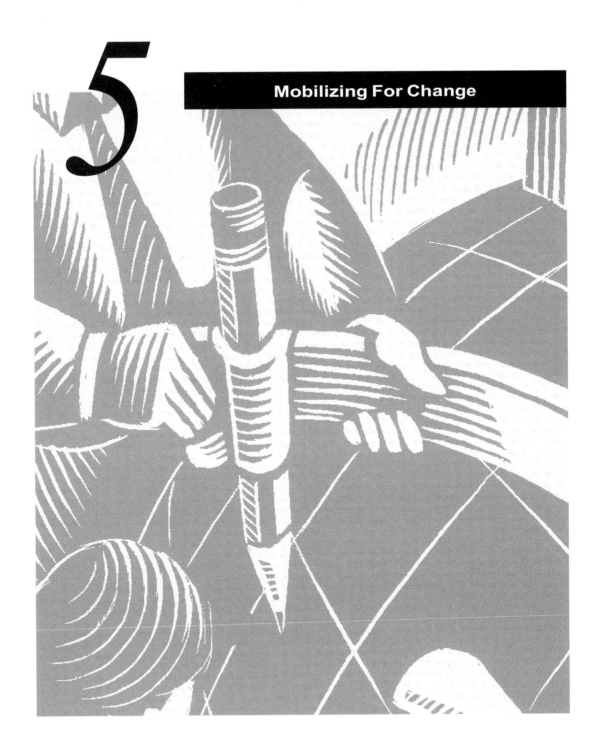

5

Define The Scope Of Change

Ownership For Change

The Change Manifesto

The Reengineering Work Plan

The Roles Of The Design Team

Mobilizing For Change

You have established a long-term plan for change and now it's time to make change happen. Chapter 9 is devoted entirely to change, but this chapter will focus exclusively on mobilization, the job of initiating change. The most important issues of mobilization are defining the scope of the change effort and assembling and preparing the people who will make the change happen.

Those who have initiated change know what can go wrong at this stage. After kickoffs christen the change effort and high expectations are set, we sometimes face the resource question and come up short. Our newly launched ships often aren't sufficiently provisioned to cross the sea to our destination.

Change agents can be their own worst enemy at this nascent stage of change. We are often anxious to initiate a change process and therefore compromise too much on resources, unintentionally dooming the effort. We think that we can get started and then come back for more resources after initial success. This usually doesn't happen, thus high expectations are matched with limited resources.

The right people with the right resources must be assigned to the project if success is to be aggressively pursued. Our rule of thumb is that the resources required for change efforts are always underestimated by at least one-fourth. Robust change designs should take a lesson from robust product

design and plan accordingly. The mobilization steps will determine the fate of
your effort. It isn't hard to identify benefits that will far out weigh the cost of
change. The hard part is the act of faith required to commit the resources
when results are not assured. Passionate belief about the need for change,
based on the gap between the current state and the organization's vision, is
required of leaders at this step. Mobilization involves these steps:

1. Define the scope of change.
2. Assign ownership for change.
3. Charter the change effort.
4. Determine the resource requirements.
5. Create organizational awareness of the need for change.

Define The Scope Of Change

In Chapter 4, the vision, mission, and principles, "outside-in" scanning, and
"inside-out" scanning identified strategic choices — that is, opportunities,
challenges, and gaps to be addressed by the change effort. In this chapter
those strategic choices are sequenced into an annual plan for improvement
efforts. The first task is to determine the scope of change for the upcoming
year. The basic decision is whether to undertake a total reengineering effort in
which all major processes and people systems are addressed, or to selectively
identify specific processes to reengineer and people systems to redesign. The
alternatives are illustrated in Figure 5.1.

Total Reengineering

The scope of total reengineering is the entire organization. The team
conducts a detailed opportunity analysis of all core processes and people

systems and develops a comprehensive set of recommendations. The steering team scanned for high potential processes and people systems. The design team will do a similar but much more exhaustive analysis. This is the equivalent of giving the organization a complete physical exam. Total reengineering makes sense when:

- Significant improvements in all core processes is imperative.
- Tackling single processes or systems is not likely to produce results.
- Entrenched paradigms and bureaucracy have thwarted previous change efforts.

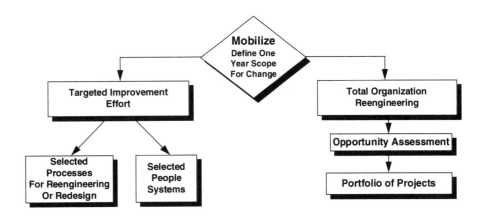

Figure 5.1 Defining the Scope of Change

The Results Expected Of Total Reengineering

The magnitude of change expected from this approach must be significant. The greatest challenge will be preparing the organization for change and successfully completing the full implementation. In a total reengineering effort, the expected results should be defined in terms of the organization's mission measures. As a result of reengineering, the organization should be in a position to achieve its three-year mission. These long-term mission measures are much better gauges of success than short-term cost-savings goals. The mission measures free the team to discover opportunities rather than simply cut costs.

Targeted Improvement Effort

The targeted improvement approach assumes that there are a few high-leverage processes and people systems that offer great opportunity for change. This approach requires a disciplined selection process. You are betting that you can significantly change some parts and substantially affect the whole. If you choose this approach, you have to be ready to broaden the scope if the leverage is not sufficient or if processes and systems are more intricately dependent than first presumed. This should not be a toe-in-the-water approach to get ready for total reengineering. If total reengineering is required, it is best to begin with it. A change effort that is too small will only frustrate and jade the organization.

Selecting key organizational processes can be guided by these criteria:
- The size of the opportunity that can be captured by addressing a process.
- The degree of challenge in addressing the process.
- The degree of risk if the process is not changed.
- The strategic significance of the process.
- The resources required.

Results Expected Of Targeted Improvement

In a targeted improvement effort, goals should be specified for each process or people system. Process goals should be stated in terms of the operation of the process, such as cycle time, and in the results produced, such as customer satisfaction. People system redesign should have similarly specific goals.

The choices of which processes and people systems to address can be plotted on a matrix like the one in Figure 5.2. Choices should balance potential impact with cost and difficulty.

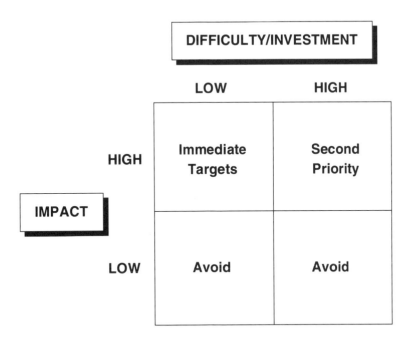

Figure 5.2 Selecting Areas for Targeted Improvement

Ownership For Change

To bring the horizontal organization to life and invigorate the change effort, assign each member of the senior team as the owner of a core organizational process or key people system. In the rush to reengineer, process owners are being established but not people system owners; people systems often remain in the shadows and untended corners of the organization. A senior manager who owns the reward-and-evaluation system should carry the same level of responsibility as one who owns the order-to-cash process.

A process or people system owner serves as the sponsor of any improvement efforts in his or her area. Some of our clients have appointed owners without building ownership into the formal reward system of senior managers and found that the concept of ownership was not strong enough. Process or people system ownership must be formalized like any other assignment in the organization. Establishing performance objectives and linking some percent of bonus to the effectiveness of the change effort will make the assignment real. The owner of the reward and evaluation system should assure that teeth are put into these ownership assignments.

The Change Manifesto

A change effort should begin with a manifesto. The manifesto is a document that answers the fundamental questions about the change. It can serve as a communication document and reference source in the middle of the change effort when participants begin to wonder why it was started in the first place. Figure 5.3 shows a partial manifesto for change. The change manifesto should contain the following elements:

- **Scope and type of change:** Describe whether the effort will be a total reengineering approach or if specific processes and people systems are being targeted for improvement. If a targeted improvement approach is selected, define the boundaries of the processes and systems.
- **Case for action:** Write a brief statement that describes the compelling reason for the effort. Describe in simple terms the opportunities and challenges that are undeniable in the environment and where significant improvement is required inside the company. Include the positive consequences that will come from success and the negative consequences that will come from inaction.
- **Link to the organization's constitution:** Include the constitution and describe how the change effort will help the organization reach its vision, achieve its mission, and live its principles.
- **Quantifying improvement targets:** Based on the improvement approach, either total or targeted, establish mission measures or specific process performance targets.
- **Scope of responsibility:** Define the boundaries of the processes and systems.
- **Overarching design principles:** In addition to the organization's guiding principles, a set of principles that describes the desired kind of organization and work processes should be created. These principles help a team design a new world that is unlike the one that Frederick Taylor, the father of scientific management, would have designed. Examples of design principles are:
    - Design the structure based on the work processes and outputs.
    - Create teams that have the largest possible boundaries of process ownership.

- Design the human environment around multi-skilled teams and individuals rather than specialists.
- Forget the functions and departments that currently exist.
- Design processes that serve the needs of customers rather than internal needs.
- Make process and customer information available in central repositories for access by any team needing to make a decision.
- Create a flat, lean, total-value organization.
- Build an organization that evidences high trust for people in all of its systems.
- Design an organization that capitalizes on the reservoir of first-level talent.
- Design a new process for turning ideas into new products.

- **Boundaries for change:** Describe anything that is sacred and cannot be changed or touched. For example, boundaries might be: "Reductions in people will not be an output of this design process," or "Pay systems will not be changed during the initial design phase."
- **Timelines and deliverables:** Describe an aggressive timeline for completing the opportunity analysis, redesign, and implementation plan of the design project.

Change Manifesto

Philosophy and Vision

- We will deliver timely, error-free, competitive services which meet or exceed our customers' expectations.
- We will be proactive and seek out customer involvement to anticipate their needs.
- We will involve our suppliers in the process of continual improvement.

Design Principles

- The design process should eliminate unnecessary or redundant activities.
- The organizational structure should allow people to take responsibility for whole processes to maximize satisfaction and responsibility.
- The new organization should maximize the efficient use of resources and people while providing the highest quality service at the lowest cost.

Boundaries

- Sound audit and control procedures must be maintained.
- The design team may redesign the method and performance basis of compensation, but not specific dollar amounts or job levels.

Timeline and Deliverables

- Improve quality, reduce cost, and shorten cycle times.
- Timeline for design teams
  - Process maps in 60 days.
  - People systems in 60 days.
  - Implementation plan in 60 days.
  - Total design time frame is six months.

Figure 5.3 A Partial Manifesto for Change

The Reengineering Work Plan

The reengineering work plan includes the major steps in the reengineering process, the projected timeline for the effort, and the resources required.

The Steps In The Work Plan

Figure 5.4 shows the steps in the reengineering work plan and who will perform them. Indicators of time should, of course, be added to the diagram. The elapsed time should be three to four months or less. Note that subteams may be formed to address specific design issues. For example, the design may determine the high-level requirements for a new pay system, then a subteam may work out the specific technical and legal issues of such a system.

The Resources Required

Typical reengineering resource requirements include:

- Four design teams.
- Overall project manager and four design team leaders (senior vice presidents).
- Steering team headed by the chairman.
- Thirty people, 3-5 days per week for three months to produce design recommendations.
- Four outside consultants.

The approximate resources needed for reengineering a small organization (2,000 members or fewer) are:

- Seven full-time team members for six months.
- One full-time experienced project manager.

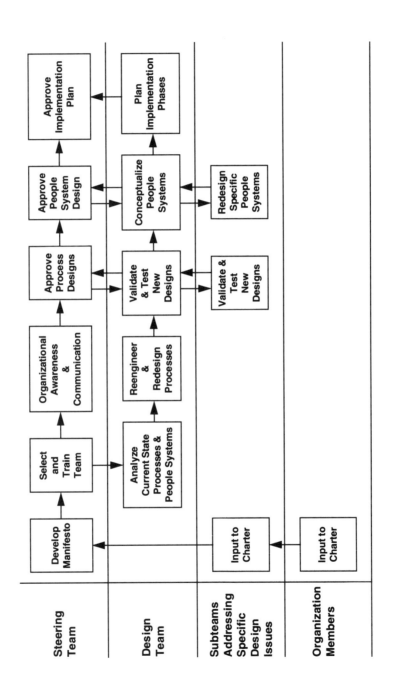

Figure 5.4 Steps in the Reengineering Work Plan

- Executive team as steering team.
- President as sponsor and coach.
- One outside consultant as a project advisor.

The Design Team

Issues related to the design team include selecting the team, identifying the roles of the team, determining the number of design teams, and training the team.

Selecting The Design Team

The issue of design team membership is complex. Some believe that members of an organization are not able to free themselves enough from their own perspective to make important changes. Thus, some reengineering efforts have been conducted by outsiders. We believe that those who work in the environment have immeasurable knowledge about what works well and what doesn't. Therefore, insiders should be the primary members of the design team. Nonetheless, outside facilitation and perspective is necessary to help the team free itself from deeply rooted paradigms. We recommend a design team of 8-12 members who represent a cross-section, including:

- Frontline associates
- Operations managers
- Key support managers
- On-call experts
- Internal consultant
- External consultant

All team members should be respected, high-performing people in the organization. Diversity is extremely important on this team. Select design team members with various experiences, backgrounds, and biases. Choose people who have become frustrated with the problems of the organization; they can now channel their energy toward positive change.

The Roles Of The Design Team

Most design team members feel simultaneously honored and apprehensive to have been chosen for the job. Team members often say that being selected represents a once-in-a-career chance to influence the whole company. On the other hand, design team members sometimes feel that they are being handed the executioner's ax, without the benefit of the mask. The latter feeling is the one to contend with. The senior team must take the burden of responsibility for the actions of the design team. The design team should not be caught between the organization's members and its leaders.

An interesting transformation happens to design team members as they design the future organization. As the future state begins to take shape, the members no longer feel the burden of the job and become enthralled with the idea of an emerging new organization. A member of a design team recently said, "I really don't want to go back to the old organization. I don't think I could live there again after what we have seen is possible."

The roles of the design team are:
- Provide input to and confirm the change manifesto.
- Push against boundaries that seem too narrow or that compromise the

case for action or the desired results.

- Develop ground rules for team dynamics and decision-making.
- Conduct current-state and opportunity analysis.
- Make final decisions on design alternatives.
- Refrain from over-specification, that is, designing jobs in great detail.
- Maintain open, two-way communication with the steering team and organization members.
- Be available, ideally on a full-time basis for 4-6 months.

Single Versus Multiple Design Teams

It is common in total reengineering efforts to assign a group of teams to reengineer the organization. When the scope is large, establishing design teams for macro processes and systems helps make the design work manageable. For example, one organization created design teams for Field Operations, Information Services, Human Resources, and Finance and Accounting. One master charter can guide the work of the design teams, but separate boundaries and design principles should be created for each team. In organizations of 2,000 or fewer members, it is common for one team to complete the reengineering assignment.

Design Team Training

A three- to five-day training experience should be planned to prepare a team for a reengineering effort. The team should be trained in methods such as those contained in this book. They should also be educated in the organization's vision, mission, and principles and the results of the "outside-in" and "inside-out" scans (see Chapter 4). The training process should also include field visits and readings about contemporary organizations.

Design Team Responsibilities

Team responsibilities include presenting and reporting to the steering team, communicating with the organization, and maintaining a healthy team psychology.

Presenting And Reporting

Use your presentations to begin changing the culture. Design teams that follow their organization's existing cultural habits for making presentations usually suffer. Often organizational cultures favor highly polished presentations that are not designed to have much genuine interaction. Often the conclusions are pre-sold and backed before the meeting. Design review meetings must be roll-up-your-sleeves work sessions. Take the initiative and set this expectation from the outset. Show work in progress and process maps with hand scrawlings and documents taped to them; do not pretty up the presentation. Use the meetings to gain the input of the steering team but do not approach the meetings with the intent of gaining approval. The design team should assume that it has been empowered to arrive at the best design given input from all stakeholders, including the steering team. When the design is complete, the steering team decides how much of the design to implement and at what rate of speed.

Communicating

The design team is the primary group responsible for managing communication to the organization during reengineering. A communication plan for both listening and telling should be developed. Listening is often forgotten, but it may be the most important aspect of communication. Do employees have an opportunity to offer input, ask questions, and react to interim analyses? Some of the vehicles for listening include:

- Establishing an anonymous e-mail box for input, questions and suggestions.
- Focus groups for opportunity identification.
- Regular briefings that include questions-and-answer periods.

One organization established what they called the "breakfast club." Leaders of the company were invited to periodic morning briefings of progress and were encouraged to take the pulse of the organization, help the team stay in touch with the day-to-day perceptions of the effort, and serve as a sounding board for new ideas.

Communication designed to tell the organization about progress should be frequent and informal. Weekly or bi-weekly updates in the company newsletter, voice mail updates on progress, and monthly all-comers meetings are ways of communicating. Keep the organization up-to-date on progress and listen to ideas and input.

Maintain Healthy Team Psychology

Design team members feel the burden of responsibility at many points during the process. Outside, pressures may continue to mount to make a difference and save jobs. Inside, the design team may doubt if the work can be completed on what is always an aggressive schedule. Design team members need to safeguard their own psychology along the path. To do this we suggest these steps:

- Meet regularly with the senior team and talk about progress and obstacles. Don't become detached and don't wait for formal briefings before talking.

- Discuss progress and concerns at the end of each day's work.

- Agree on what should be communicated to the rest of the organization from each week's work. This is necessary to assure that team members are "going public" about the same topics and keeping other topics private until they are further developed.

- Take a break and recharge. The design team facilitator must stay in tune with the energy level of the team. Vary the task assignments, work in small groups, and change locations to keep the energy level of the team high.

- Check your biases and assumptions. Discuss images of the new organization that are emerging. Even while mapping the current state, ideas begin to emerge about the future organization. Encourage this creative thinking and periodically brainstorm wild ideas for the future. Save these ideas and use them when you are designing the future organization.

- Check team dynamics and conduct teambuilding before it is needed.

- Use props to poke fun at the organization's sacred cows and the team's own biases. One team had a sacred cow mascot that could be trotted out any time a team member was resisting an idea in favor of an old practice or assumption. Such efforts maintain a light, humorous atmosphere while pointing out when "old thinking" rears its head.

The Roles Of The Steering Team

The steering team is the senior management team of the organization.

The role of the steering team is to provide leadership for the reengineering process. In addition to defining the future (see Chapter 4), the steering team drafts the change manifesto. The manifesto includes a) the scope and pace of the design effort, b) the case for action, and c) specific objectives and boundaries for the design team. In addition, the steering team provides feedback on the design team's recommendations, and helps the design team with ideas for the design and implementation plan as needed. In addition, the steering team should:

- Provide training, information, theory, and technical expertise.
- Refrain from expert solutions or making decisions reserved for the design team.
- Be available for all planned meetings with the design team.
- Conduct organization analysis as required, prior to the design team's work.
- Be a learner throughout the process.

Preparing To Lead Change

After a senior team has initiated a reengineering effort, there is a great deal of work to be done with the senior team itself if the implementation stage is to be successful. Unfortunately, the senior team often initiates the effort then waits to hear the results of the effort. During that time, the design team evolves significantly in its views of what is possible. The design team begins to live the future while the steering team continues to live in the current state. The senior team needs to have similar experiences if they are to be ready to lead the implementation when it is complete. A one-day session once a month that allows the senior team to further develop leadership skills, dream about the future that they want to create, and discuss concerns will help to make the implementation effective.

Fast-cycle Process Redesign

Some of our most successful efforts have involved compressing the time required for process redesign. The concept of cycle-time reduction can be applied to the improvement effort itself. In several cases, we have successfully trained a process improvement team and facilitated the redesign of a process within one week. This compressed, think-tank approach maximizes the concentration of the design team members and obviously speeds the pace of the overall effort. This approach requires these prerequisites prior to the session:

- Data collection on process performance.
- Customer analysis and customer feedback.
- Interviews with key stakeholders.
- Preliminary current-state maps completed.
- Availability of key resources (before and during the week).

6

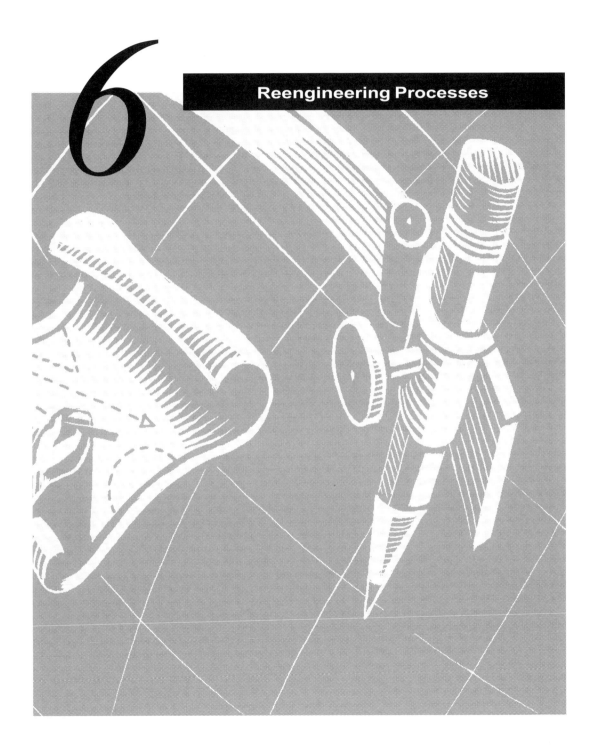

Reengineering Processes

6

What Is Reengineering And When Do You Do It?

Reengineering Is Not Continuous Improvement

The Steps In Reengineering

Reengineering Processes

The purchasing function was disintegrating. Other departments wouldn't use the function and there was great concern that high prices were being paid because no one was taking advantage of volume buying opportunities. Groups that should have been internal customers of central purchasing had developed their own supplier contacts and price structures because the centralized purchasing function was slow, operated with too many rules and restrictions, and had lost touch with its internal customers. Purchasing was trapped by old rules, antiquated systems, and a complete lack of understanding of how fast opportunities appeared and disappeared in the market.

There are two ways to handle a situation like this. The traditional way would be to issue an edict requiring everyone to use purchasing or suffer dire consequences. The assumption here would be that purchasing, now unthreatened for its survival, would work on improving. The result however would most likely be frustration among its customers.

The other way to handle it would be to "blow up" the process and start over with new assumptions and work-design models. New questions offer new possibilities. How can groups do their own purchasing and still take advantage of volume buying? Could the purchasing function be turned into a database of supplier choices? What if goods were paid for when received, eliminating the cumbersome step of matching purchase orders, packing slips, and invoices? All of these options are possible with a reengineering mindset.

Reengineering Around Us

You don't have to look very far to find many examples of reengineering. When your local gas station installed credit-card processing equipment on the gas pump a process was reengineered. Work that was formerly done by someone else, somewhere else, is now done by the customer. Customers even like doing the "extra work" of processing their own credit cards because it saves time and avoids standing in line. Retailers like the speed at the pump, allowing more people per hour to buy gas.

Most of us don't go inside a bank much anymore. Studies show that young people who weren't introduced to indoor banking go into a bank once every few years. In addition to ATMs, loans are processed over the phone and personal bankers go to your place of business.

In everyday life there are certainly ways to get rich if you could reengineer certain processes. The process of doing the laundry could stand some work. The technology stops at the drying step just when the most tedious and laborious work — folding — begins. The latest efforts at reengineering have moved to the upstream side of the process with the design wrinkle free-clothes — new slacks developed by Farrah and Levi's Dockers.

These examples illustrate that reengineering is about changing the *what* of work, the product or service itself; the *how* of work, technology and work methods; the *where* of work, anytime, anyplace; and the *who* of work, suppliers and customers take over parts of the process.

What Is Reengineering And When Do You Do It?

This chapter is designed to give you a method to follow as you act on the organization's change manifesto. Reengineering is a little like giving an organization a brain transplant. When processes are reengineered, the organization will think and act differently. People will have a view of the business from end-to-end and customers receive higher-value products and services. But, do you need the radical surgery of reengineering? This is worth pondering, because once you begin it is hard, if not impossible, to turn around.

Some common indications that reengineering is in order:

1. **People are always bypassing the clogged artery.**

    For example, the new product development process isn't really capable of developing new products; it churns along modifying current products. When something really new is really required, a new group under separate management is formed to do the task. New products don't come out of new product development but out of special, "off-line" task forces. These could be called "virtual teams" for product development if the company really intended to design products this way. More often, it is a bandage to a basic process problem.

2. **Downstream processes have built elaborate screens and double checks to handle defective input.**

    For example, a manufacturer sets up elaborate front-end screening to catch raw-material defects because lower-quality supply is so much cheaper. On the assumption that cost savings on raw material are greater than the cost of the added checking steps, a whole process is turned into "checker central."

3. **Centralization and decentralization are debated on the basis of who will control the resource.**

For example, services that could be easily centralized are fought against because managers do not believe that the current culture will allow people to stay focused on the customer. The sentiment in the field is that headquarters will have people working on things that don't matter to customers and the field will get stuck with more work. The fear is that headquarters will grow and expect more from the field as the bureaucracy's needs win out over customers' needs.

4. **Customer service representatives are set up as a shield or expediter for customers to mask the complexity of internal process.**

It all seems to make sense on the surface. By putting someone in charge of a customer's order we can be sure that it will get done right. Often this is only done for a few big important customers that can't be subjected to the normal, convoluted process.

5. **Real work time is out of proportion to the total time that work is in process.**

Claims in insurance companies typically take thirty minutes to process but take thirty days to get through the maze and back to the customer. Work has been so segmented that more time is spent batching and waiting than working on the task. Stalk and Hout have documented the typical disproportion of process time and real work time and developed the "5% to .05%" rule, which holds that most input is actually worked on about 5 to .05% of the time that it is held hostage in the process.

6. **Voice mail has become the major way of communicating to avoid missed hand-offs and to assure that expected work is done.**

   The fact that voice mail allows people to talk anytime doesn't mean that better, faster, and more cost-effective work processes are being operated. It may mean that voice mail has become that ultimate checker's checking system.

7. **Knowing who to work through is more important than knowing how to work the process.**

   If calling in old chips and knowing who to talk to is the best way to get work accomplished, it is a sign that the whole system is broken and needs a lobotomy.

Reengineering Is Not Continuous Quality Improvement

At a recent reengineering conference many presenters described how "reengineering" really was just a new word for what they had already been doing. If it's the same, what is all the fuss about? Thomas Pyzdek has written that he can find the roots of reengineering in every aspect of total quality management and has urged quality practitioners to stay the course and not change or add methods.

Two things seem indisputably true with respect to this subject. First, reengineering offers several new tools and a decidedly new mindset. Second, if your organization isn't moving rapidly toward the realization of its vision, its time to get a new horse that runs faster and on a different track. Our belief is that the most successful efforts under the TQM umbrella were successful because the tenants of TQM were applied comprehensively and, upon a platform of continuous improvement, fundamental processes and structures were changed.

Several criteria define reengineering. One of the following two criteria must be met in reengineering:

1. The change effort addresses an entire organization including all core processes and people systems, or
2. The processes and people systems targeted for reengineering are core processes and are defined so that they cut across current organizational boundaries.

Reengineering projects should be noteworthy because they make big changes in work processes, outputs, and business results. Reengineering should:

1. Change the outputs that processes produce.
2. Change how the output is produced.
3. Change the flow of work and the interplay between groups.
4. Simplify and consolidate work that has been broken apart.
5. Shift work to suppliers or customers.
6. Use new technology to enable any or all of the above changes.

The final test of reengineering is in the business results and increased value supplied to customers. In reengineering we expect to see dramatic improvements in performance by orders of magnitude. This expectation is the single most important distinguishing factor of reengineering.

Fix It Or Flail At It

Several years ago Roger Smith, then chairman of GM was asked why he hadn't gotten tougher and fired more people. His reply to *Forbes* was "O.K., we could do that, and it's the way we used to do it. But the Fisher man says 'Wait a minute. I did my job. My job was to fabricate a steel door, and I made a steel door, and shipped it to GMAD. And it's GMAD's fault.' So you go over to the GMAD guy and say, 'Listen, one more lousy door and you're fired.' He says, 'Wait a minute, I took what Fisher gave me and the car division's specs and I put them together, so it's not my fault.' So you get the Chevrolet guy, and you say, 'One more lousy door, and...' 'Wait a minute,' he says, 'All I got is what GMAD made.' So pretty soon you're back to the Fisher guy, and all you are doing is running around in great big circles."

Roger Smith did a lot of running around in great big circles during his tenure and had a hard time making a substantive difference. Trying to fix part of a whole process can feel as fruitless as Smith describes it. Unless we work on a whole process that cuts across the boundaries that are built into the workflow, everything makes sense in the context of something else, even when the whole thing makes no sense at all.

Roger Smith also gave us several good lessons about the limits of technology. The most technologically advanced plants in the GM system could not compare in cost or quality with the NUMMI joint venture with Nissan in Fremont, California. NUMMI was the worst GM plant before management operations were taken over by Nissan who turned the plant around without new technology, but with lots of state-of-the-art thinking about work process improvement, teams, and new paradigm management.

Radical Not Conservative

At a reengineering conference recently a group of executives from an insurance company presented their work on reengineering. The presentation was entitled "Risk Management and Reengineering." The presentation offered a cautious risk-avoidance orientation toward reengineering. Every chance of something going wrong was enumerated and studiously avoided. The approach was so cautious that one can hardly imagine how anything important could be changed. The approach was truly culture-bound. Would the results have been different had the approach been called "opportunity maximization"? Since reengineering begins on paper, we can be radical, crazy even weird. Caution has no place in reengineering. It should be a courageous, but not foolhardy, endeavor.

New Rules

It is important to remember that reengineering should be radical. It is reinventing part or all of your business. From the outset, the intent is to break the rules and discard old assumptions we have about how best to accomplish work. We should examine our assumptions and beliefs to break traditional work paradigms.

Current rules trap our thinking. We are often unaware of the rules we are following. We are stuck on the "who" and "how" of work. Consider the customer billing process. If we accept the "who" and "how," we work on typing invoices without errors and mailing them within one day of an order. If we break out of the "who" and "how" assumptions, we can see the process as getting cash from the customer's bank account to the company's bank account and we can set up an electronic transfer process. If we redefine the assumptions of the relationship, we may have customers send money based on what they receive with no invoice at all.

Following traditional rules, no one would expect a senior executive to waste time making his or her own travel plans. These should be communicated to an assistant who works with a travel agent and offers options to the executive, who then makes choices. In a reengineered world, today's technology allows the executive to make plans and spend even less time than before on the entire task. We now see executives making their own flight plans by computer rather than through secretaries. Decisions about where to go, when to leave, and where to stay are made in real-time. Steps are eliminated, time is saved, and desired choices are probably available more often. This is a simple example of reengineering, but it is reengineering nonetheless because the boundaries of the process were changed, and the nature of the way work is accomplished was changed. A process that once involved a secretary and a travel agent has been reengineered so that one person can do the work in a few minutes rather than a few hours.

Under the rubric of reengineering, many are just tweaking processes — polishing the brass in the same old mansion as the foundation decays and the roof rots. Michael Hammer, the father of current reengineering thinking, offers these principles to distinguish reengineering from other improvement efforts:

1. Organize around outcomes, not tasks.

2. Have those who use the output of the process perform the process.

3. Subsume information-processing work into the real work that produces the information.

4. Treat geographically-dispersed resources as though they were centralized.

5. Link parallel activities instead of integrating their results.

6. Put the decision point where the work is performed, and build control into the process.

7. Capture information once and at the source.

In addition, a set of general principles can be drawn from Thomas A. Stewart's *Fortune* article, "The Search for the Organization of Tomorrow:"

1. Organize primarily around process, not task.

2. Flatten the hierarchy by minimizing subdivision of processes.

3. Give senior leaders charge of processes and process performance.

4. Link performance objectives and evaluation of all activities to customer satisfaction.

5. Make teams, not individuals, the focus of organization performance and design.

6. Combine managerial and nonmanagerial activities as often as possible.

7. Emphasize that each employee should develop several competencies.

8. Inform and train people on a just-in-time, need-to-perform basis.

9. Maximize supplier and customer contact with everyone in the organization.

10. Reward individual skill development and team performance instead of individual performance alone.

The most dramatic level of reengineering is literally redefining the business. A company may change the nature of its products and services so that it redefines the business it is in, and opens up many new possibilities. In one reengineering effort, the initial scanning revealed that customers wanted real-time information rather than printed books. New processes were designed to make electronic information available, and suddenly the company was in the on-line-information-availability business rather than the publishing business. We may extend the boundaries of the company upstream or downstream and thus change the definition of the business. A trucking company may extend downstream and operate warehouses, or a shoe manufacturer may do what Nike has done by stopping its processes at product design and outsource the manufacturing process. Nike is now a service company that designs and markets apparel.

The Steps In Reengineering

Reengineering spends little if any time on the current state. Instead the focus is on creating the state-of-the-art. We may look back over our shoulder at the current state to check for anything good that shouldn't be left behind, or to compare relative performance, but we will blaze forward to a new process. This is a significant departure from process improvement where processes are studied extensively to find places where time can be captured and waste and errors reduced. Although exhaustive current-state analysis can uncover many nuggets of improvement, reengineering focuses on a radically different future state. We will describe current-state analysis when we discuss process improvement in Chapter 7.

Our experience is that the first step should be to focus only on the outcome we wish to produce and analyze the essential transformations, not activities, required to create the outcome. Spending too much time on the current state can lead to what Michael Hammer calls building the "six-sigma buggy whip company." When we start a project by saying, "Let's begin as if this company were starting its business today," we can create new processes built on new assumptions.

Figure 6.1, first presented in Chapter 2, shows the methodology we are following. This chapter takes the block entitled "Process Reengineering" and explodes it into a sequence of steps. Figure 6.2, which was also first presented in Chapter 2, describes the reengineering steps and the desired outcomes of

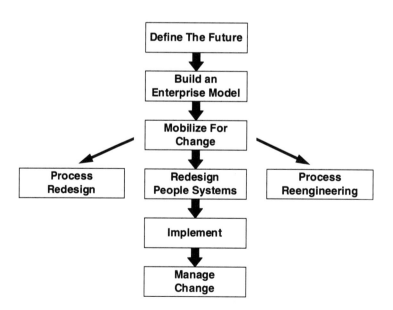

Figure 6.1 Reengineering Methodology

each step.

"Customers don't want

quarter-inch drills;

they want

quarter-inch holes."

A Black & Decker

customer service

maxim

1. Redefine The Output

We start reengineering by thinking of possible redefinitions of the output. The first mental set we will break is the one that assumes that the outputs, products, and services of our processes are the ones we need to be producing. We will take the opportunity at this first step to change everything, beginning with the outputs themselves. To rethink the outputs of our processes we can ask ourselves these questions:

- What is our product, free of its current physical form?
- What does our product accomplish for the user, or said another way, what state or condition does our output create?
- What more can be attached to the output to increase its value to customers.

Completely separate from its current physical form, what are the most basic core elements of our product? For example, when a supplier of financial and business information looked at its output from a form-free perspective, they redefined the output as financial information. An output conceived as information for daily decisions, not published manuals and news reports, leads one quickly away from stagnant once-a-year manuals to live, on-line information. A virtual financial manual, always up-to-date, that the user can access anytime becomes the output rather than a fixed book that begins aging the day it is published.

For a beverage company, the product can be obviously defined as the physical product in a can or bottle. To broaden the definition, the output

*"Don't pedal faster,
redesign the bicycle."*

may be defined as a refreshment experience which suggests many other outputs as part of the value package. Similarly, a beverage supplier can define its output as matching the customer's order. If the definition of the output is broadened, the beverage company can supply the customer with demographic preference information so that the customer can order what sells well in an area and has the highest profit potential. Is the output just the product, or the value-added information that lets the customer make money and give consumers what they want? Certainly it can be both.

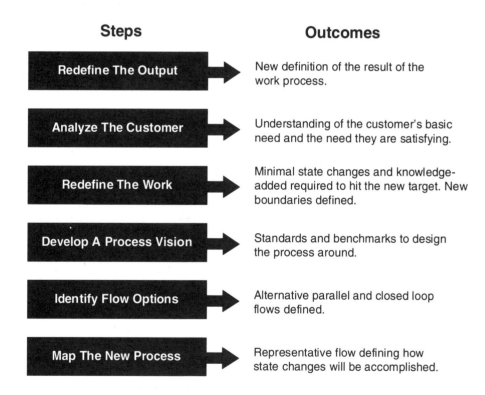

Figure 6.2 Process Reengineering: Specific Steps

American Express has broadened its definition of the products it supplies to retailers. Not only can they supply card service, the credit card use data allows American Express to provide, for example, a restaurant chain with a database of its most frequent customers as well as other customer profile information. With this information, the restaurant chain can market to its loyal customers and know how to attract new prospective customers that fit the loyal customer profile. American Express is supplying customer information to restaurants as much as it is supplying credit card access to restaurant goers.

The examples illustrate how often we remain constrained in our thinking based on the form that we have given to our product or service. We can add significant value to our current outputs by redefining their forms and adding other elements to the outputs.

These are other examples of the current form of an output followed by a reconceptualization of the output:

Fixed books:	· Decision-making information
Consumer products:	· Profit-making potential
Television:	· Information access
Service repair:	· Fixed equipment

Another way to reconceive our output is to consider what it is supposed to do for the customer. A way to think about this is to consider the *condition* that the output creates. A payroll process may define its output initially as a check to employees. If we ask what condition this output intends to create, we think about "money in an associate's bank account" as the output. From a new output definition, a new process can be defined that takes pay information and transforms it into an electronic deposit in the associate's bank account.

Saturn has reengineered many of its processes, including how inventory is managed. Saturn reconceived the output of the inventory process by asking its suppliers to redefine their output as a constant state of inventory. In this instance, the output of the inventory supply process has been redefined as "sufficient inventory to keep the production line operating without interruption." The output from the supplier company is no longer a specified number of gears matching a purchase order but a condition called "We don't run out." Redefining the output also redefined the responsibility for keeping the right level of inventory. Suppliers took on the task of inventory management when they were made responsible for the end condition.

Many suppliers now say, "We'll be sure that you don't run out," as a way of adding value and differentiating themselves from competitors. That is the condition that the output is intended to maintain. To do this, process boundaries change as well. The supplier must look inside the company's inventory system to determine when shipments of raw material should arrive. The amount of resource devoted to tracking inventory, ordering, and checking for correct arrivals is eliminated and customers can pass along better prices to customers.

2. Understand The Customer

Understanding the customer should occur in tandem with redefining outputs because it is almost impossible to think about one without also thinking about the other. Understanding the customer goes beyond understanding customer requirements for the current product. It means understanding *why* customers need the output and what requirement *they* are working to meet.

We do not begin by looking inside the process. Rather, we look at the output we provide from the user's perspective. Further, we examine why the customers need what we provide in relation to what *they* do with it and what *they* provide to *their* customers. This perspective allows us to reconceptualize the output of our process.

The most important lesson and limitation in defining customer requirements is that customers tend to tell you what they want based on what they have or have not gotten in the past, and based on their current view of what you should supply them. Customers typically help us understand how to hit an existing target. When the target is redefined, the basis of the customer-supplier relationship changes. Even in the best spirit of quality thinking, working to hit the customer's current target can lead to the maintenance and entrenchment of current broken processes. One reason reengineering needs to encompass several work boundaries is to be sure that the team can throw out interim requirements — the requirements of interim steps that may not need to exist.

In the example of financial information services, a combination of redefining the form of the output as information (rather than as a book) coupled with understanding the essential customer requirement led to a reengineered process. Ford reengineered its invoice payment process by meeting a requirement that suppliers would never have thought of because it threw out old sacred rules about proper billing and receiving. If Ford had asked vendors what they wanted they would have said that they wanted to have their invoices paid in thirty days or less. They would never have offered the target of throwing out invoicing and being paid electronically upon receipt of goods.

Understanding Your Customer's Customer

An important step to take in understanding the customer is to take the advice of Deming and Drucker and be sure that you understand your customer's customer requirements. In Figure 6.3 a simple diagram can be turned into a worksheet for doing this analysis. This exercise will reveal how much, or how little, you know about the "why" of your process. After all, it exists only because of what it helps the customer do farther down the process stream.

3. Boundary Redefinition

In process definition, we are asking three basic questions. They are

1. What are the upstream boundaries of the process?
2. What are the downstream boundaries of the process?
3. What is the essential work to be done to produce the output?

The answers to these questions will force examination of the beginning and ending points of the process. Our objective is to define new beginning and ending points for the process. Then we can look inside the process to simplify the essential work to be done inside the new boundaries.

Downstream Boundaries

At what point is the work done? We look to see if the downstream

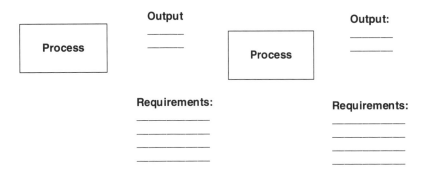

Figure 6.3 The *Customer's* Customer's Requirements

boundary can be moved so that more or less work is performed in the process itself. When a manufacturer learned that some final assembly steps are better done after installation by the customer, they moved the work downstream.

If the final steps in the process are the least value-adding, we may be able to move them downstream. Can the customers configure parts into a customized product, such as writing their own book by selecting from available electronic chapters and printing the book themselves? If so, much of the work of printing and binding has moved downstream, and incidentally, the total value of the output has probably increased. A customized book is much more on-target than the fixed package that would have been available.

Upstream Boundaries

Can our suppliers do more of the work of our process? Wal-Mart asks suppliers to take much of the responsibility for its inventory and pricing processes. Process boundaries overlap organizational boundaries, offering opportunity for both customers and suppliers. The implications for partnerships and sole-supplier relationships based on quality and trust can be explored.

State-changing Work

Value-adding is the vocabulary of essential work. To analyze the real
work that is required in a process, it is important to have a conceptual model
that lets us forget how the work is accomplished today and rethink how to
produce the outputs. The cleanest method for doing this is to understand state-
changes.

State-changes are what happens when value-adding work occurs in a
process. It is a state-change because the input is actually transformed. By
beginning with an understanding of the minimum number of state-changes
required to complete the transformation, we can stay out of the trap of doing
the work as it is done today. We want to focus on the essential transformations
that the input must go through as it becomes output. Then we can consider
what activities need to be done in the process.

In the enterprise model shown in Figure 3.5, we defined processes in the
From/To construction. The From/To construction uses state-change language.
For example, the total state-change in a process might be from customer order
to installed equipment. The task in reengineering is to determine the fewest
number of interim state-changes required in the total transformation.

Under the glare of state-change analysis, it becomes clear that most steps
in a process don't change anything. No wonder real work is only happening
5% of the time. Most of the work is not changing a state, it is creating a state

of confusion. Approvals, double-checks, waiting in a batch, and reentering data into disconnected databases do not accomplish any real work according to the state-change model.

To follow the logic of state-changes, we do not focus on what should happen to the input on its transformation journey or how the state-change should be accomplished. In the examples of an order becoming an installed piece of equipment or a lead becoming a customer, we should first ask if the state-change can occur all at once without interim states being created.

Consider an invoice payment process. The process of turning an invoice into a payment in most operations currently involves several steps, including checking the invoice against the purchase order and the packing slip and entering data into the inventory and accounting systems (which may not be linked). Without state-change thinking, we might think of how to do each step better. With state-change thinking, we can ask ourselves if the whole state-change can be accomplished in one operation. In this example, payment made electronically to a vendor's bank account is the answer to this state-change challenge. The meaningful state-change — received order to paid supplier — happens in one step.

Manufacturing processes are easily thought of in state-change terms. In a steel mill, scrap metal goes through several state-changes. The first is from scrap metal to molten metal, the second is from molten metal to alloy-rich molten metal, the third is to from molten metal to being formed into hot billets, the fourth is from hot billets to cool billets, and the fifth is from cool billets to rod. The technology that accomplishes these state-changes should not be mentioned as the states are identified. A reengineering team will design processes that eliminate interim state-changes and accomplish necessary state-changes.

Chapter 10 provides more step-by-step instructions and offers a format for doing state-change analysis.

Taking Work Out Of The Middle

Often as we look at a macro-level process, we can see that there are many points where products are aggregated and distributed again. In traditional product distribution, intermediate holding points are numerous and add no value. A manufacturer may produce product at a plant, move it to a regional warehouse, load it into trucks, take it to distribution centers, unload it, and load it again on a local-route distributor truck. The numerous loadings and unloadings are often so institutionalized — after all, the company owns the buildings and the trucks — that it is hard to see that steps in the middle could be eliminated.

4. Develop A Process Vision

What is the state-of-the-art for this kind of work process? Benchmarking against the best in the world should come next. When we have understood what we need to provide, we can begin to establish standards of excellence. How much, how fast, against what standard will process excellence be judged? What available benchmarks of excellence are available?

Process Measurement

Another way to think about the boundaries of a process is to redefine the measurement boundary. The measurement question is, "How do we decide what the ultimate effectiveness of the process is?" For example, in human resources we may define the boundary on the hiring process as the point at which a new employee is on the job for ninety days. A longer boundary may be placed on the measurement of the hiring process by tracking turnover of employees in the company under three years. This measure would reflect to some degree the effectiveness of the hiring process.

Technology Options/Enablers

With the minimum number of state-changes identified we can look to technology to perform the necessary operations. We also want to explore technology to remove the centralization/decentralization argument by centralizing data and decentralizing decision. Decisions can be made in the field if current data is available to anyone, anywhere.

5. Methods Of Workflow

There are several workflow options to consider as we reengineer a process. Henry Ford and Frederick Taylor gave us division of labor, sequential work, and specialized steps as the standard workflow. Other ways to consider workflows are as follows:

Parallel Interactive Flows

Our traditional workflow model is the sequential flow of work. Incoming material is sent to department *A* for the first machining operation, then to *B*, *C*, and *D* for each essential operation. In a similarly traditional fashion, a marketing plan is often conceived and hatched long before sales people ever see it. The Ford Taurus is the most trumpeted example of a work process in which parallel processes was employed. Simultaneous engineering can be executed through involvement and effective communication, or by changing the work itself is accomplished. A complete work cell is an example of the latter.

Work Cells

The most celebrated work cells were the well-publicized experiment at Volvo's plants in Sweden. This approach became an excessively costly way of manufacturing a car, and the experiment was terminated. The concept though should not be discarded. The idea of constructing work teams as independent cells that have all of the skills and resources to complete a whole job is compelling. Cycle times and quality improve in work ranging from insurance claim processing to new product development.

Single-person Whole Process

Some call this the "case approach," adopted from insurance companies that have case managers who can handle everything related to a claim. Can individuals become sufficiently multi-skilled so that they can operate whole processes independently?

Other questions to consider as we plan optimum workflows are:
- What activities should be accomplished simultaneously?
- What knowledge needs to be available to everyone in real-time?
- What work should happen in parallel?

6. Mapping The New Process

Fleshing out the precise workflow of a reengineered process can be done by the design team, or ideally, by the people who will be doing the work. When designing how work will be accomplished at the level of the operating team, follow the maxim of Albert Cherns, one of the pioneers in work redesign, who offered the principle of "minimal critical specification." Minimal critical specification means that process designers should specify only what is absolutely necessary, allowing process operators to tailor the process to local operating conditions with their expertise and experience.

Chapter 10 offers methods for mapping current-state and ideal processes. Whether done by the design team or work team, the essential step is to map in detail how the work will be accomplished. If operating teams have good blueprints to follow so they can continually improve, chances are the reengineering effort will not go up in smoke.

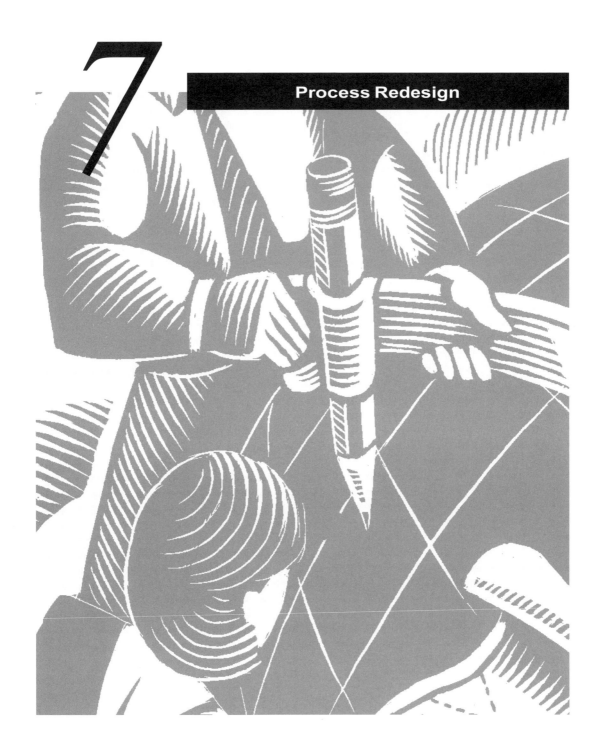

7

Process Redesign

7

The Characteristics Of Work Processes

The Steps In Process Redesign

Process Redesign

Process redesign and ongoing process management are the two key elements of this chapter. These are the two phases of the ongoing work of a permanent operating team. Process redesign activities are a regular part of the team's work, and process management keeps processes from degenerating after they have been improved.

The cycle in Figure 7.1 shows the sequence of tasks involved in process redesign and management. To operate this cycle, each team begins with a common understanding of the organization's vision, mission, principles, and strategy. Upon this foundation, the team defines its unique performance

Figure 7.1 The Continuous Improvement Cycle

promise. A performance promise is the negotiated agreement between the team and its customers about the outputs to be produced and the requirements to meet. The team then works to deliver on its promise and evaluate how closely performance matches the original promise.

Process redesign is the final step in the cycle and occurs when the team analyzes its process for improvement opportunities. The continual process of improving work flows has two intended effects:

- Improved economics and effectiveness of process operation.
- Improved capability of the process to deliver a better performance promise in the future.

Process redesign is an analytical approach for identifying improvement opportunities. By looking at an existing process, within its existing boundaries, the team accepts its current scope of process ownership and looks for improvement opportunities. This approach assumes that the outputs of the process are right and that the customers will benefit from a team improving its hit rate relative to the target that the customer has established.

Process redesign and ongoing management: a) provides a common language and way of addressing problems; b) is a concrete, preventive approach to continuous improvement; c) makes work easier and more efficient; and d) enhances cross-functional teamwork.

Process redesign and management represent a systematic approach to improvement. It gives teams a practical model and set of tools for analyzing and redesigning their work. Process thinking is based on the ideas that:

- Results occur the way they do — good or bad — because a process (including people, procedures, materials, and equipment) has evolved that is producing them.
- To change the results, you must change the process.
- Processes tend to maintain themselves unless actively changed.
- People cannot improve results (in spite of pressure or rewards) unless the process is improved, because people are but one element of the process.

Process redesign does produce significant results. *Fortune's* Thomas A. Stewart reported that the act of mapping the process of making turbine shafts at GE's Evendale, Ohio plant resulted in "...a 50% time saving in 1991, a $4 million drop in inventory, and a good shot at getting seven inventory turns a year versus 2.6 before." Similarly, a team at Motorola reduced the number of steps in the invoicing process from 16 to 5, reducing time to process from 3.6 days to 30 minutes, which resulted in a total reduction of cost from $30.71 to $10.

The Characteristics Of Work Processes

Most work methods, job definitions, and organization structures were defined in organizations before the advent of process thinking. For this reason, the paradigm of process thinking must first be adopted by a team before significant improvements can be made. Historically, work design involved breaking a whole job into individual tasks. This task model of work produced job specialization and necessitated a management approach based on high control and close supervision. The net effect was that processes were rarely

137

improved by any change that was made. Changes to correct something that was going wrong typically involved further specializing or adding more check and control steps. Every time something happened that "should never happen again," a rule, procedure, or safeguard was institutionalized. With this approach, processes became encumbered with many steps that add no value and make no sense in the eyes of those who operate the process or those who receive its outputs.

In order to achieve the full benefits of reengineering and keep processes from degenerating after reengineering, all operating teams must have a full grounding in the philosophy and skills of process redesign. This view allows a team to adopt whole-process thinking even if it owns a part of a larger process. To apply these improvement methods, an operating team will need to:

- Develop a process mindset about work.
- Map its work as a process.
- See the process from the perspective of the customer.

Understanding Value-added

A commonly used but not well understood concept is that of value-added. The economic equation of value added is significantly simple: the cost of the input plus the cost of the process must be less than someone is willing to pay for the process or the process is not adding sufficient value. Those activities and steps in a process that transform, change, or add to the input in a way that brings it closer to the customers requirements can be described as adding value. Steps that guard against error, sort out defects, and double-check do not add value in spite of any strongly stated "need" for these steps. Based on the current construction of a process, the steps that are not value-adding may be necessary but could be eliminated with a different process construction and people paradigm.

Processes And Time

Most work processes have lost all track of time. Often, the amount of time that work is "in-process" has nothing to do with the actual time required to accomplish the task. In their seminal work analyzing the relationship of time elapsed to time actually required to do the work, George Stalk, Jr. and Thomas M. Hout developed several fascinating rules about the consumption of time as work processes are operated. The authors developed the following rules of thumb:

The .05 to 5 rule.
The 3/3 rule.
The 1/4-2-20 rule.
The 3 x 2 rule.

Most companies find these rules of thumb to be true when they put their processes under the glare of these analytical lenses. Insurance companies, for example, find that the .05 to 5 rule applies to the insurance claim process. The real work time involved in processing a claim is reported to be about 30 minutes while the elapsed time that the claim is in process is typically 30-60 days. The relationship between actual work time and total time elapsed have gotten completely out of proportion.

Almost anyone analyzing a company's work processes will find something akin to this rule. James Sierk of AlliedSignal, commenting on his company's process improvement efforts to *The Wall Street Journal* observed, "We found that actual work was happening 10% to 20% of the time we were spending to make a product. The rest was being spent on waiting for materials to arrive, papers to be signed." Sierk's analysis gives his company a better ratio of total time to real work time, but the room for improvement is still enormous. Take a process you are familiar with and apply the same basic analysis and see what you find.

Briefly, the other rules are defined as follows. The 3/3 rule says: time spent waiting is equally divided among 1) waiting for completion of work of which the product is a part, 2) waiting for physical and intellectual rework, and 3) waiting to send the batch on to the next step. The 1/4-2-20 rule says: for every quartering of speed, the productivity of labor and working capital doubles and costs reduce by 20%. The 3 x 2 rule says: growth rates of three times the industry average and profit margins of twice the industry average result from increases in speed. Speed as a driver of improvement is a powerful tool for wringing out the non-value-adding steps of a process. Just considering how the process would be different if it operated twice as fast as it currently does will generate many ideas. We will return to this idea in a later section.

When To Use Process Redesign

Teams use the improvement cycle as a prompt to step back from the day-to-day operation of the process to conduct a regular team meeting and evaluate process operation and the degree to which performance promises are

"If you wait to correct a problem until the next stage in a process, the cost of fixing it goes up ten times."

A rule of thumb at Hughes Aircraft

being delivered upon. Gaps between performance promises and actual delivery and gaps between process goals and actual performance cue the team to look at the process for improvement. Teams will employ the skills and tools of process improvement when the process:

- Does not deliver products or services desired by the customer.
- Produces variable and unpredictable results (quality, cost, or speed of products and services).
- Has no flexibility against customer expectations and requirements.
- Does not produce what the customer wants or expects.
- Adds no value for the customer.
- Is done by people without the necessary skills or information.
- Creates rework.
- Is done with inadequate or misused equipment.

The Steps In Process Redesign

The method outlined here links back to the overall model we are following in this book. The steps in process redesign are as follows:

1. Process definition.
2. Understanding customer requirements.
3. Current state mapping.
4. Process analysis.
5. Identifying improvements.
6. Mapping the ideal state.
7. Defining measures and management.

1. Process Definition

At this initial step in process redesign the work process itself must be defined. Process definition involves clearly identifying:

- The process output.
- The name of the process.
- The beginning and ending points of the process.
- The customers of the process.
- The inputs to the process.
- The suppliers of input to the process.

Begin process definition by completing the worksheet in Figure 7.2.

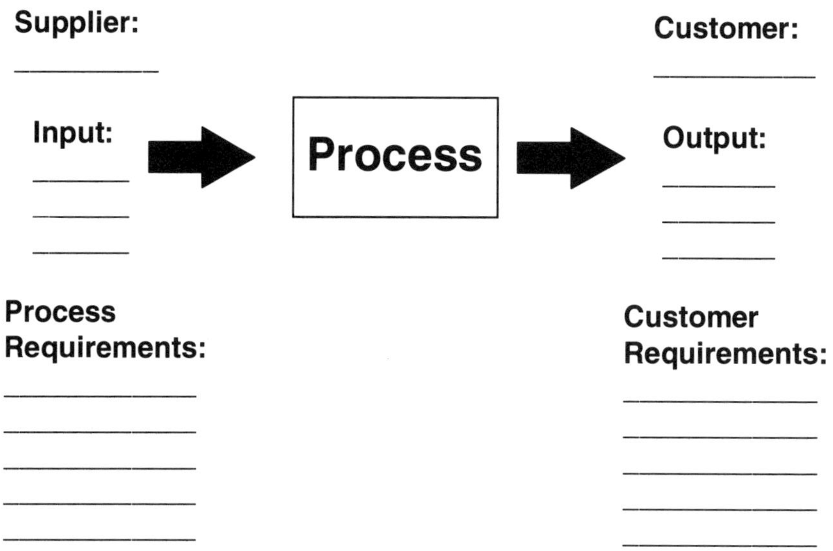

Figure 7.2 Process Definition Worksheet

After completing the initial definition of the process, the team should check to be sure that the process is being addressed in the most holistic fashion possible. It is worth considering stretching the boundaries upstream or downstream to include other teams so that a larger process can be explored.

2. Understanding Customer Requirements

Once the process has been well defined, it is essential to understand the customer's requirements of the outputs of the process. Requirements define quality and service from the customer's perspective. Requirements should be written from the perspective of the customer and written in language that customers would really use. Avoid the technical jargon that only the producing experts would recognize. It is helpful to define requirements into two categories: must-have's and like-to-have's. Requirements, once defined by the team, must be validated with real internal or external customers. (See *Continuous Improvement: Teams & Tools* by the authors for more detail on developing pinpointed customer requirements.)

3. Current-state Mapping

Current-state mapping is often the starting point for teams when working on a process. The tendency is to think that the boundaries and requirements are common knowledge that don't change much, but time can be wasted mapping processes that aren't well defined, and developing improvement ideas that don't improve the process from the customer's perspective. Complete Steps 1 and 2 thoroughly before mapping the current-state of the process.

Process mapping is different from traditional work flowcharts.

143

Oftentimes traditional work flowcharts:

- Are done only when a process is first designed.
- Are done without input from those doing the work.
- Describe what someone *thinks* happens, not what *really* happens.
- Are not used to examine the requirements of both people and workflow.
- Are not used to look for performance breakthroughs.

Process mapping is the technique of using flowcharting to illustrate the flow of a process, proceeding from the most macro perspective to the level of detail required to identify opportunities for improvement. It's what Geary Rummler calls "peeling the onion." Process mapping focuses us on the work rather than on functions and hierarchy. Often called the "as-is" or "current-state" flow, it provides a snapshot of the existing process in terms of:

- The critical activities in the process.
- The sequential connection of these activities.
- The information flow through the organization.
- The time and cost of each process step.
- The major relationships with other process flows.

The purpose of this step is to map the current-state but not to memorialize the current-state. As you map the current-state, be aware of the pitfalls of digging into the "as-is" process. Usually a five- or six-step macro map will provide sufficient detail to identify process problems and stimulate improvement ideas. When the current-state is mapped out in great detail there is a risk that all of the steps will be justified, lest everyone acknowledge that the process is a wreck. Process operators who have done the work for a long time will sometimes explain all of the steps of the process in a way that completely justifies the current construction.

Developing a detailed current-state map will be most helpful when team members have difficulty coming up with improvement ideas based on a macro map. The detailed relationship map helps by showing what a plate of spaghetti the process has become. In one case, a design team mapped an equipment installation process and found that the process touched 12 different groups and had 50 steps to take a customer order and have equipment installed at a customer location at a desired time! The equipment removal process was even more complex. Upon seeing the detailed maps, a senior executive exclaimed, "It's amazing we ever get a customer a piece of equipment, and we know why we get so little of it back." The labyrinth of 50 steps across 12 functional groups, with all its intricate glory, was more complex than anyone knew. The case for change was made by the detailed map. The educational value to groups who owned parts of the process was great. Everyone who did some part of the process was aware of what they needed and what they delivered, but had no conception of the complexity of the whole.

Current-state Mapping Methods

There are several mapping methods for displaying a process. The methods we will describe here and in more detail in Chapter 10 are the:

1. Macro block map.
2. Relationship map.
3. State change map.

Macro block map. A macro flowchart, or macro map, illustrates the handful of birds-eye level steps in the process. This high-level view allows the team to see the high-leverage process steps and to ask, "What can vary at each step that will cause variability in the process output?" The example in Figure 7.3 shows a macro map of a hiring process. In this case, the hiring process has three macro steps. Increasing amounts of detail can be shown by mapping each step of the process.

Figure 7.3 A Macro Block Map of a Hiring Process

Relationship map. If a number of teams and individuals touch the process, use a relationship map to identify the hand-offs. A relationship map is a process map that shows *who* performs each step in the process. Relationship maps can dramatically illustrate illogical aspects of a process, such as unnecessary movements or the poorly timed involvement of an individual or group. Figure 7.4 shows a relationship map of an order-taking process. The map shows the steps in the process as well as who performs them.

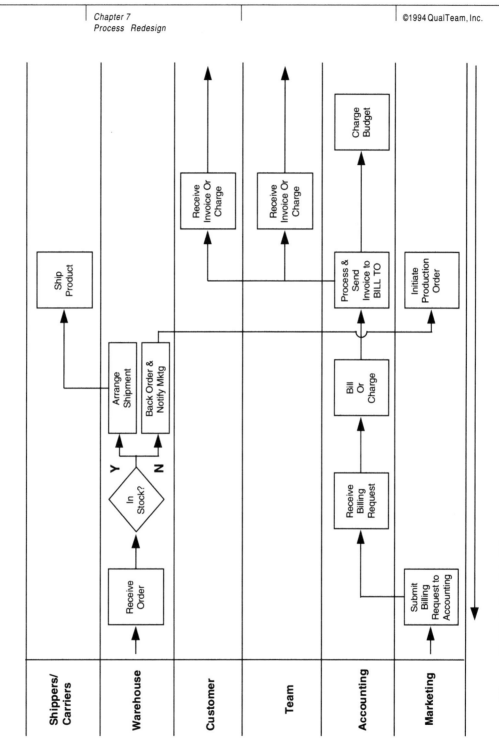

Figure 7.4 Relationship Map

4. Process Analysis

Once the current-state has been mapped, we can analyze the work. The major methods we will use to analyze the current-state are:

- Process performance data.
- MACS (Massively Applied Common Sense).
- Variance analysis.
- Cost and speed analysis.

In process analysis, we want to know where the big opportunities for process improvement are. We don't want to jump to the most obvious things that are bothering the team, rather we want to take the time to find the high-leverage problems that will mean the most to our customers when removed. Process analysis searches for the inherent variability that has been built into the process.

Process Performance Data

Before making improvements in the process, a team should examine the quantitative performance data of the process. The steps in analyzing process performance data include:

- Identify information that is currently available about the process, including the volume and quality of output, the cost and speed of the process, and customer feedback.
- Identify what additional data would verify your intuitive sense of the causes of variability.
- Collect and display the data. Analyze the data to verify the actual causes of variability in the process.

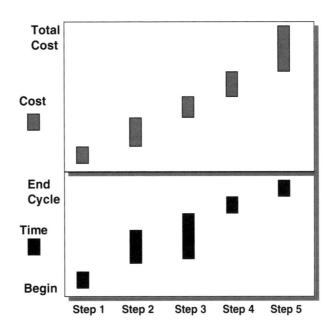

Figure 7.5 Cycle Time and Cost Analysis

A tool like the one in Figure 7.5 is a helpful way to display speed and cost data. The speed half of the chart shows the time per step and to what degree the process is a linear or parallel flow. The cost half of the chart shows the cost per step and the cumulative cost of the total process. The two views of the process let us see opportunities for improving the parallel flow of the process (to reduce cycle time), and for reducing the costs of the individual steps (to reduce the total cost of the process).

Whole Process Scan

This section offers several angles on analyzing a process. Each thought is then exploded into specific questions a team can ask as it looks at its process:

- Does the team structure support process operation?
- Do we have accidental bureaucracy?
- Are we duplicating our work?
- Can we simplify?
- Can we save time?
- Can we standardize?
- Can we better utilize tools and equipment?

Does The Team Composition Support Process Operation?

- Is a process owner identified?
- Is the team composition appropriate to accomplish the process steps?
- Do we have smooth interaction and communication among team members in accomplishing the process steps?
- Do we have smooth hand-offs and information flow with the suppliers and customers of the process?

Do We Have Accidental Bureaucracy?

- Do our policies and procedures support process goals?
- Do we have redundant inspections or unnecessary sign-offs?
- Do we have task interference, where bureaucratic requirements prevent people from accomplishing their true mission?

Are We Duplicating Our Work?

- Would it help to have owners in charge of specific process steps?
- How about owners for particular process measures?
- Can we establish or improve central files?

Can We Simplify?

- Can we simplify our language, particularly when communicating with customers and suppliers?
- Can we keep paperwork simple, such as putting forms on one page with instructions on the back?
- Can we avoid asking for data, reports, and responses that we know we don't need?
- Can we eliminate completely unnecessary steps?

Can We Save?

- Do we have bottlenecks or delays? Do we know where they are?
- Can we perform steps in parallel rather than serially?
- Have we collected data on the causes of our delays?
- Have we challenged ourselves to cut process cycle time in half?

Can We Standardize?

- Do we have templates or boilerplates for the routine, repetitive aspects of our work?
- Have we defined how we are going to communicate with each other (content, method, and frequency)?
- Have we benchmarked among ourselves on the best ways to do our work?

Can We Better Utilize Tools And Equipment?

- Is there any equipment that would save time, reduce mistakes, or help us help our customers?
- Would new computer software, or training on existing software, help?
- Would new computer hardware (such as modems or scanners) help?

- Would tracking process performance in a spreadsheet or database help to improve the process?
- Have we only partially embraced the electronic world, causing our processes to remain inefficient?
- Is there sufficient availability of tools, checklists, and other job aids?
- Can we upgrade people's skills in using our equipment?
- Does the physical layout of equipment facilitate the work?

Massively Applied Common Sense

Using a relationship map to show the process steps in detail, apply these common sense questions to spot improvement opportunities at each specific steps:

- Can we eliminate this step?
- Can we combine this step with others?
- Can we perform steps at the same time rather than in sequence?
- Can we complete each output rather than batching at each step?
- Is this step in the right order?
- Can the supplier or customer do this step?
- Can we do this step in a different way?
- What assumptions about process design led to this step?
- What could be done upstream to allow the elimination of this step?
- What can go wrong at this step?
- If this step goes wrong, what is the impact on the output and on the customer?
- How long does this step take?
- What is the cost and time of this step?

- What errors can be created at this step?
- What can happen at this step to delay the output?

Variance Analysis

Another way to look at a process is to consider its variation. We begin by working backward from the output and asking how the variation in the output against customer requirements can be affected by variation in each of the process steps. In the process of assembling a car, for example, variation in the strength of a weld can produce variation in stability or quietness of ride.

A variance analysis diagram allows the team to identify what can vary at each step in the process and cause further variation downstream and in the output. Variances are first identified using a macro map. In Figure 7.6, the

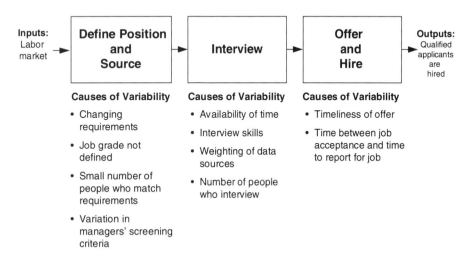

Figure: 7.6 Macro Block Map for Variance Identification

macro block map of the hiring process has been repeated and includes the results of brainstorming the "causes of variability" at each macro step.

These possible causes of variation can be prioritized if there are several at each step. Then the variances are analyzed in a variance analysis matrix, such as in Figure 7.7, to determine which variances do the most downstream damage in the process. We will call these "key variances."

Process Steps

Legend:
- ↑ High Correlation = 3
- → Medium Correlation = 1

Process Step	1	2	3	4	5	6	7	8	Variance
Take Order	1								Incorrect Name
		2							Incorrect Order
			3						Wait to Enter
Pick Order				4					Out of Stock
		↑			5				Wrong Order
				↑		6			Incomplete Order
Pack Order							7		Wrong Package
						→		8	Poor Packing
				↑		→			9 Partial Packing
					↑		→		10 Partial Shipping
Label & Ship	↑								11 Wrong Address
		↑							12 Wrong Shipper
	↑	↑	→						13 Late to customer
								↑	14 Damaged Goods
		↑		↑			→		15 Incorrect Order Received
Key Variances	6	12	1	9	3	2	2	3	

Figure: 7.7 Variance Analysis Matrix

To develop the matrix, list the macro process steps down the left axis. Then list each of the variances along the stair steps on the right side of the diagram. For each variance, look down the vertical column and ask, "Does this variance cause the next variance in the sequence?" We can use a simple scoring system, using the up-arrow to indicate a direct cause and a side-arrow to indicate a partial cause. If we give each arrow a point value, we can see that the variance "Incorrect Order" in Figure 7.7 directly causes four other variances in the process. "Incorrect Order" receives a score of 12 and is the most significant variance on the chart so far. Using 80/20 thinking, we can select the upstream variances that create 80% of the problems downstream and feel confident that we are solving the root causes of process problems.

Another step that can be taken in variance analysis is to correlate key variances with key customer requirements. This method looks at the significance of the variances in relation to customer requirements. Figure 7.8 shows a worksheet for this analysis. The correlation between variances and requirements can be a final check of the most important variances to control or eliminate. Other process analysis tools are presented in Chapter 10.

5. Identifying Improvements

To identify ways of redesigning the process while controlling variability, and measuring process performance, we suggest the three approaches here. The first is to develop ideas based on maximizing a given process driver. A second method is to develop ideas based on maximizing a given principle. The third approach is to find solutions for key variances.

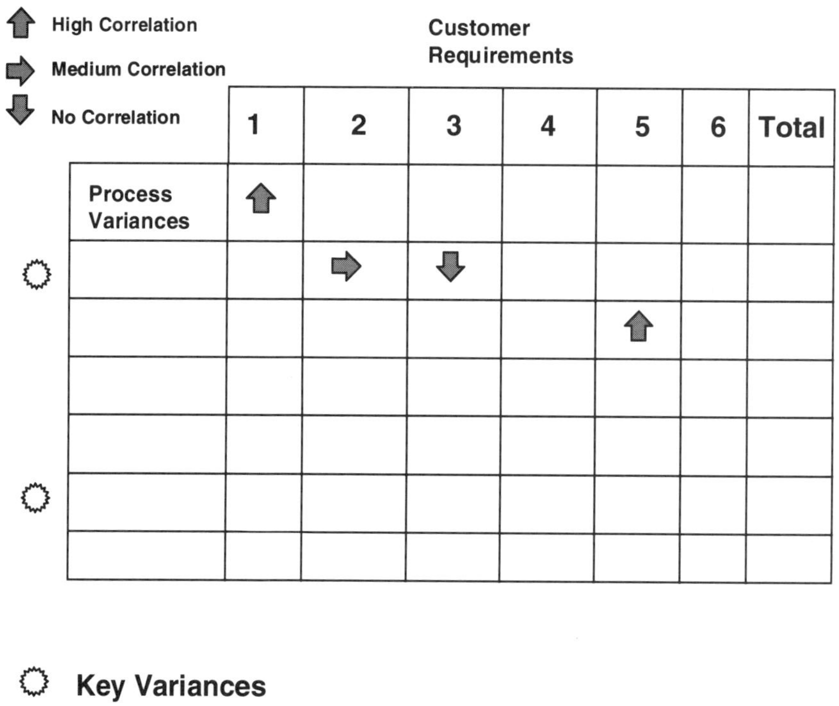

	High Correlation			Customer Requirements				
	Medium Correlation							
	No Correlation	**1**	**2**	**3**	**4**	**5**	**6**	**Total**
	Process Variances	⬆						
○			➡	⬇				
						⬆		
○								

○ **Key Variances**

Figure 7.8 Variance and Requirements Correlation

Maximize A Driver

Drivers are critical dimensions of the process, such as quality, cost, speed, and customer satisfaction. Ideas for improving the process can be generated by asking questions such as:

• How could we double the output?

• How could we cut the error rate in half, half again, and so forth?

• How could we double the speed?

- How could we eliminate customer complaints?

Maximize A Principle

We can look at a process and consider how we would optimize a given organizational principle such as:

- Keeping decision-making as close to the customer as possible.
- Maximizing responsibility for the operator.
- Encouraging the fewest hand-offs from the order to the customer.

Eliminate Variances

The key variances that cause the greatest downstream variation and variation in the process should be eliminated. By narrowing variances down to the critical few, a team will be able to generate solutions for eliminating the variance.

6. Mapping The Ideal State

Incorporate the improvement ideas into an ideal state process. Beginning with a clean sheet of paper, begin to map the process flow (typically a relationship map is used). The team should incorporate as much detail as possible into the map. The map will be the guidebook for team operation once it is complete and will be used to orient new team members. New ideas should be validated and incorporated into the map so that slow degeneration does not occur.

7. Defining Measures And Management

How will process performance be measured on an ongoing basis? What we recommend is to develop two sets of measures: process output measures and process variable measures.

Process output measures. Process output measures are measures of the outputs of the organization or team's work processes. Process output measures are used to track the products or services of an operation. Examples of process outputs measures are number of requests processed, number of projects finished, and number of projects meeting deadlines.

"Remember to think of upstream process improvement rather than downstream damage control."

Process variable measures. These measures track the performance of the process before outputs are produced. Often, the results of the variance analysis offer keys to process variables to track on an ongoing basis. Examples of process variable measures are the number of calls answered within 20 seconds, the temperatures of the ovens in a baking operation, and the time taken to produce first drafts of proposals. Every process variance should be dealt with by eliminating the variance, designing process steps to control the variance, or tracking the variance to be sure that it remains within acceptable control ranges.

Finally, the team should establish a regular review cycle for the process using the performance measures. Establishing a management process that follows the Promise, Deliver, Evaluate, and Improve cycle will assure ongoing improvement and provide a base for growth as a team.

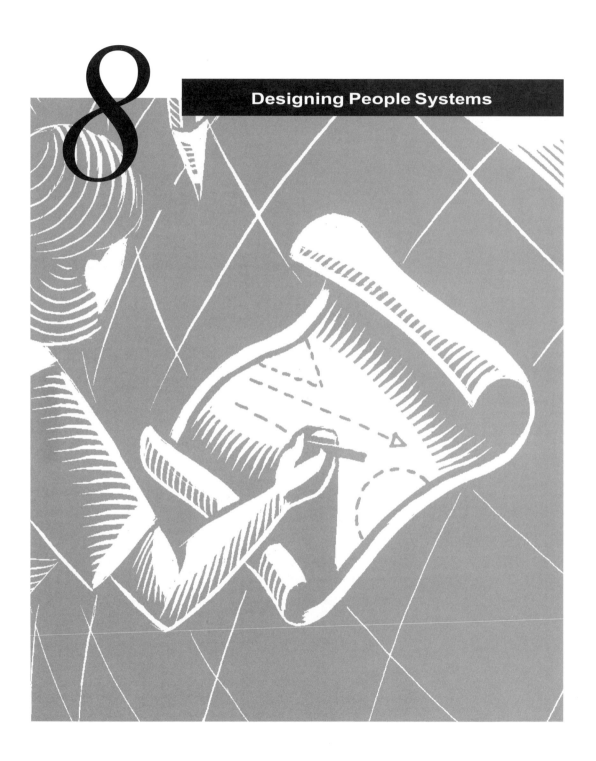

8

Designing People Systems

8

Designing People Systems

This chapter begins by examining some of our assumptions about work, motivation, and job design. The intention is to encourage the organization designer to think deeply about the kind of workplace to be designed before plunging into the tasks that will affect the worklife of every associate. Without serious thinking in advance of the task, we build systems, structures, and jobs without having a clear vision of the work environment we want to create, and a well defined set of assumptions and principles on which to base design decisions.

In the next several sections we will examine why we work, what motivates us to work, and how we design workplaces and jobs. The next 15 pages will, hopefully, help stimulate a vision of the workplace that matches your highest aspirations for what work can be. The people system methodology will be described in the remainder of the chapter.

The Evolution Of The Job

Work is ultimately about how we live the largest part of our daily lives. Work is the daily getting-up, readying kids, sloshing down coffee, and trudging through the nine-to-five routine that dominates our lives. While people once worked just to survive, the concept of a job is, as William Bridges notes, a relatively new idea. Only a hundred years ago work was not compartmentalized into a block of time. In 1900, ninety percent of Americans worked in some aspect of agriculture, and "nine-to-five" had not yet been conceived.

Bridges argues that the job as we now know it is going away again. This is supported by the fact that the boundaries that limit work by time and place are being obliterated. Instead of returning to the agrarian job model, we are creating the cyber-space job model with voice mail, e-mail, and computers at home that allow work to be done anywhere and at any time. For some, this is the ultimate liberation: being able to work when work makes the most sense in the most pleasant environment.

Others don't think the trend in the workplace is good. Charles Handy laments about the changing job scene: "The Chairman...summed up his policy very neatly...1/2 x 2 x 3 = P, half as many people in the core of his business in five years' time, paid twice as well, and producing three times as much, that is what equals productivity and profit." This model becomes problematic when the ability to produce more is based on the willingness of associates to continue adding hours to the work week.

If corporate prosperity requires family disintegration, then our progress as a culture is illusory. The challenge in the workplace is to design work processes and supporting environments that are people friendly, productive, and creative. This is not necessarily the tone of the day set by many organizational leaders. One senior manager of a company where 80-hour work weeks are common told of his conversation with the company president who observed that people in the organization just needed to work harder. "Work harder?" He explored, "Don't you mean work smarter." "No," replied the president, "I mean just that, we need to work harder."

Many hard working people are working 80 hours per week for largely internal reasons. Rewriting reports, running another set of numbers before the meeting with the bosses boss, and other poor reasons for not seeing your spouse or kids, make up many of these hours. In the world of knowledge-work, the idea that re-work is waste hasn't gotten very far. Demanding bosses use the idea of continuous improvement as a license for capricious change, and endless re-work is part of the normal work process.

Why Work?

As jobs emerged in the early industrial revolution, people worked primarily to survive. We have left behind this period when our job was to assure that basic needs were met and now we work for so many other reasons. While most people would say that they work only because they have to, they would also say that they expect a job to supply much more than food and shelter. A job should be a vehicle for growth, both personally and in terms of lifestyle. The challenge in designing people systems is to create an environment that allows these objectives to be met.

In designing people systems, it is helpful to imagine the kind of work place where people would want to work even if they didn't have to. The demographic fact of life is that the highly-prized and skilled workers of the future will increasingly have the choice of several jobs. When the choice of whether to stay with a company rests more heavily with the associate than the company, a significant power shift occurs that changes the workplace dynamic completely. In the future, managers must become architects of desirable workplaces rather than decision-makers about who stays and who goes.

163

As we design the people environment we should have in mind our daughters and sons who may one day work for the company. This image will help us design a state-of-the-art work environment that will first attract high performance people and then cause them to stay and prosper. The current fact of organizational life is that it gets harder and harder to attract and keep good people for at least four reasons.

- People will quickly leave jobs for better opportunities elsewhere.
- The available pool of high skill people will shrink over the next twenty years.
- More and more people are leaving large corporations to start their own businesses.
- People entering work today are likely to have at least five different careers.

Good For People Or Good For Business

In Rod Serling's classic business film *Patterns,* there is a dramatic scene in which the senior management team addresses the upcoming purchase of a business. The plan, as proposed by the general manager, is to purchase the company, shut down its operations for six months for modifications, then open it again after changes are made. The assistant general manager objects to the plan on the basis that laying off the 800 plant employees for six months without pay or assurance of a future job will cripple the village, destroy goodwill, and leave the plant weakened or unable to operate. The assistant general manager's position is blasted by the CEO as, "Entirely non-corporative and highly charitable...little beyond the tongue clucking stage." And he is beaten into submission for not having "...Anything resembling an analytical point of view that serves the needs of the business first."

This piece of film has stirred many debates in our seminars. Most side with the "soft" manager because his rationale has a business-base. Some, generally more senior managers, side with the autocrat feeling he has a good line of reasoning and that he is just a little strong in his delivery. The polar opposites represented in the two views describes the paradox of people concerns and business concerns that we seek to resolve.

One way of looking at the paradox is characterized by, "What's good for the business is ultimately good for the people," so let's do what is good for the business first. The other view says, "If people get hurt along the way, it is ultimately bad for the business," so let's make sure people concerns come first. Today, with many organizations bloated with bureaucracy and plagued by slow processes it often seems that there are no good choices.

The Darwinian principle of organizational survival says that any organization which accumulates fat, inefficiency, and wasteful practices over a period of time with little competition will face a day of reckoning. For some organizations, IBM most notably, it is as if they awoke like Rip Van Winkle from a twenty-year slumber to a changed world where they are ill equipped to live.

For those who have faced their reckoning and survived, the stories have a mixed lesson. Mike Walsh, while serving as president of Union Pacific Railroad, spoke dispassionately about eliminating six layers of management in order to create an organization that could act on its intentions. The number of people who lost their jobs is not part of the story. *Business Week* rightly applauds how Rockwell Corporation has changed its business focus from military to commercial, and rung up significant profits as seven levels of management were eliminated. The lessons in these cases are often described in terms of the bravery and wisdom of the new leaders who made the hard decisions, and they do deserve tremendous credit for making tough, but necessary, choices. What is lost in the lesson is why the previous management ignored changes and emerging trends, and allowed their organization to grow to such a state of ineffectiveness that such harsh measures were required.

The lesson of leaders who can right a listing ship are obvious, the less obvious lessons are from the period of decline. As one of the original founders of Jostens commented after the company went through its first layoff ever, "...layoffs ultimately represent the failure of management." As we witness the hundreds of thousands of layoffs happening in business today, we see the evidence that leaders now must anticipate how the new drivers of the value era will impact their business, and quickly build the organization that can prosper in these new times. Learning to change large organizations in enough time to avoid catastrophic consequences, and building people systems and work environments that prepare people for the demands of a changing world, inside or outside the company, are the leadership requirements of the day. We can do what is good for the business, even if it means reducing its size, without compromising the good of people if we have prepared them with a range of skills for a changing world.

Liberals And Conservatives

The cosmic struggle between practices and choices that are good for the business or good for the people are often pitted against each other as the liberal

"Joy in work is anybody's birthright."

W. Edwards Deming

and the conservative points of view. In our western way, we tend to use three kinds of logic to determine which of the two polar opposites, the people or the business, is most important. We are prone to think about complex issues by using logic founded on dichotomy, linearity, and reductionism.

Dichotomous thinking seeks the one element that is most important. We see good and evil, black and white. This logic is often supported by linear or dependent logic that argues, if A comes before B, then A is more important because B can't happen without A. This is often the same logic that argues for the superiority of one function over others. "If we didn't sell products you guys in manufacturing wouldn't be able to do your job," the argument goes. A third kind of thinking is reductionism. We want our issues reduced to a common type so they can be dealt with independently. People issues are dealt with separately from business issues, process issues or finance issues. Interdependencies are complex and troublesome. To deal with the "good for people, good for business" choices we need to adopt synergistic thinking where we don't think in terms of trade-offs but, think of joint optimization. To design the optimum workplace, we will have to find the synergy between what works well for people and what works well for processes. Finding the synergy will ensure superior performance and satisfying work.

The sociotechnical school of Emery, Trist, and Cherns was the first to argue profoundly that optimum systems, as Deming advocated, occur only when the conditions that are best for technical and human systems are jointly planned. This notion should drive the design of the human environment. It's not which comes first, or which is most important, but how to have the best business that is also a great place to work.

Joint optimization carries with it several elements that are less than obvious. One is that the people of the organization will be treated as full scale adults that are most satisfied and effective when they are fully engaged, growing, and learning. Deeply rooted in our historical assumptions is the basic model of employee as child and manager as parent. The parent is here to maintain order and to mediate the rewards and punishment from the outside world. We all lose when we see the corporation in the parent role because the inherent idea is that the children need protection from the harsh reality of the world. After protecting the "children" for a long time, leaders are often surprised at the shock of associates when leaders decide to start treating them like adults who can handle reality.

When we create environments that assume the full adulthood of associates we minimize the number of rules, checks and supervision required. We have to leave the military and school system models behind in this new workplace. New workplace thinking, and demographic reality, would argue that a business may be doing well in profits, but if it is doing poorly in the attracting and retaining associates, its prospects for future success are low.

A New Motivation Equation

Creating a new workplace begins with new ideas about the characteristics of a high performance environment. One of the old premises of our post-industrial revolution model of business had to do with the nature of motivation. At one time motivation was based on the most basic needs for a job. The need to provide food and shelter kept men, women, and even children working in times past.

As our society evolved, and we moved past a subsistence level of thinking about motivation, we began to build a motivational model based on the premise that people need to feel that they are advancing if they are to continue to work hard. Thus was born the period of pay and promotion as the primary motivational tools. A good employee should be rewarded with a higher base wage and a promotion at predictable intervals. The net effect of decades of applying these motivational levers was to increase layers of management and produce pay levels that grew out of proportion to the business reality. Pay and promotion need to be replaced as the primary methods of motivation. To do so, we need to understand some of the basics of motivation.

Internal Or External Motivation

When theorists discuss motivation there is much debate about whether the strongest motivation is internal or external. Ed Deci and Alfie Kohn have argued that externally-oriented sources of motivation, like praise from your boss, decrease the inherent reinforcing value of the work itself. When such external motivators are used, they reason, the worker is more likely to be oriented to the rewards than to the job. On the theory argued by Deci and Kohn, any reward meted out by the organization is likely to reduce the overall motivation level of the workforce.

There is an opposite view of motivation that contends that motivation is a function of the positive and negative consequences provided by the environment. Based on this theory, managers should "catch people doing good" and look for opportunities to provide positive reinforcement and corrective feedback. Kohn, Deci, and others would argue that this kind of consequence management decreases overall motivation and commitment to the job. We agree with this contention, but on different grounds. It is easy to focus on whether rewards are good or bad, internal or external, and miss the main point, which is whether the consequences to behavior are authentic — that is, based on the reality of the environment.

The undisputed fact of life is that the environment dispenses consequences for all of our actions. New products are successful or fail, sales proposals win or lose, and similar consequences follow all of our work endeavors. The big issue of internal versus external sources of motivation isn't so much about what is inside and what is outside, but how accurately the outside world is reflected. In more technical psychological terms, we might say that management has taken on the role as mediator of the natural consequences of the world, softening or accentuating the world's consequences as good judgment warrants. Perpetual parent-child relationships exist in this model and motivation does suffer. If we adopt an adult-to-adult model for developing rewards and feedback at work, we eliminate the role of manager as regulator or modulator of feedback and rewards, and allow the natural consequences of work to be experienced. We all feel the effects of success and failure in our stomachs and in our wallets.

As an example of experiencing "real consequences," the craftsman who loves his work is "managed" by the unseen customer who will use his product.

When the external consequences of a job come to govern behavior even in their absence, as in this example, we tend to call the craftsman internally-motivated. The cause of his motivation is the combination of natural consequences that follow from the results of his work—his customers give positive or negative feedback, not his boss. The issue is not that the motivation is internally- or externally-based, but whether or not the consequences of performance are authentic and experienced.

There are two conclusions to draw from this section. First, we can increase internal motivation by designing systems that make sure that everyone experiences the authentic consequences that the environment dispenses. This happens when everyone receives feedback from their immediate customer and performance feedback from their teammates. In addition, we seek to link individual compensation to organization and team performance.

Secondly, the most powerful element of a new motivation equation should be designed *into* the job. A major source of internal motivation must come from the nature of the job itself and the degree to which it is reinforcing to produce the work output. Today we have the double win opportunity of designing jobs that are more satisfying, and at the same time prepare people with an array of skills that prepare them for a changing world.

A New Approach To Motivation

Other elements that satisfy the motivation equation of the value era include:

Purpose: A strong, shared purpose reflects what is important about the work of the organization. Each individual finds meaning in work through a purpose that is stated in the vision, mission, and principles of the company. Leaders live by and model this purpose. Purpose also comes from a clear understanding of one's important contribution to the products and services of the company.

Reward and recognition: Formal and informal systems reward performance that is consistent with the organization's purpose and principles. Job designs maximize the sense of personal satisfaction and self-control. Reward systems reinforce team and individual performance and are based on the consequences in the external environment.

Involvement: Every member of the organization is a member of a team in the most complete sense of the word. Teams have a responsibility to deliver on their performance promise and employ all of the skills and abilities of team members toward that end. Involvement comes from regularly engaging in problem-solving and team meetings. Involvement is also fostered through open sharing of information.

Development: Associates have the chance to learn new skills and grow within every job. Learning is a prominent characteristic of the organization.

Empowerment: Teams have a clear and meaningful responsibility to make decisions that are best for the customer and best for the business. Teams are empowered to improve their process and meet the requirements of their customers. Bureaucracy is minimized and speedy decisions are made. People are treated as the responsible adults they are.

Taylorism Revisited

Designing workplaces can't occur without paying a final visit to the work of Frederick Taylor and the factory of Henry Ford. Most workplaces today are based on many of the ideas that were popularized during the heyday of the industrial revolution. Assembly line production, job specialization, and management for control were primary outputs of this period that have endured far too long.

In 1905, the Ford factory looked less like a factory as we know it today and more like a craft shop. The craftsmen of Ford's factory worked together, much as our self-managed teams do today, to build a car. As Ford sought improved methods that would allow more cars to be made more cheaply, he came under the spell of the consulting guru of his day, one Frederick Winslow Taylor. The difficulty that Ford had encountered was that the production process was slow and costly. Cars would not be affordable to the people who were employed to build them unless costs could be dramatically reduced. An automobile cost about $900 in 1908, far too much for the worker to afford to buy. Taylor had an answer.

Taylor's imprint on his era, and on the American psyche up to this day, was profound. He was a breakthrough thinker who exploited Adam Smith's basic idea of division of labor and helped to transform Ford's craft shop into an assembly line. Over several years tasks were repeatedly broken into smaller

"This organizational

model we got from the

German army and the

Roman Catholic

Church gets us very

confused about who

works for whom. The

truth is that the

manager works for the

people who work for

the customers."

James L. Barksdale,

AT&T

divisible parts and with each succeeding division came an increase in line production and a decrease in costs.

Taylor, ever the student of work methods, sought the one best way to accomplish any task and then standardize that method across all workers. The early work that made Taylor famous included an analysis of the work of men shoveling coal. After experimenting with various work loads, Taylor found that the ideal shovel load was 21.5 pounds. When this level of load was used, 140 men did the work of 400. In another experiment that analyzed men moving pig iron, he found that if the worker rested 57% of the time, output more than tripled. The results were irrefutable. Taylor became the messiah of efficient production. Output went up and resources employed went down. Jobs became mindless, brains would henceforth be checked at the door, and the craftsman was replaced by the drone.

The success that followed for Ford and his factory was tremendous. The cost of a Model T went down to about $200 within a short period of time and the car for the masses was born. The rest, as they say, is history.

The imprint of Taylor has yet to be extracted from our psyche when we think of the best way to get work done. Taylor's philosophy about people doing work has also been hard to shake. As David Halberstam has noted, "...Taylor, had an abiding disbelief in the enthusiasm of the average worker for his chores..." Mechanization and specialization ruled the day. Ford followed Taylor's lead and became an advocate of assembly lines and job specialization. Ford was fond of saying, "Shoemakers ought to settle on one shoe, stove makers on one stove. Me, I like specialists." The remnants of this era were narrowly-defined jobs, and assumptions about people that required parent-child style management.

Remember Your Worst Job

Lastly, before designing the people environment it may pay to reflect on a period when you were just starting to work. We sometimes feel that the awful things we survived in our work career have earned us the right to inflict similar rites of passage on others. So, as a last preparation, think about a job you had that you hated, and one that you loved, before you design a state-of-the-art workplace.

One of the authors remembers a job that set him on the path in search of a better way to work. This "worst job" was a summer job during college working for the first time in a factory environment. The factory made bathroom fixtures including old-fashioned wooden pull-chain toilets. The job at *Heads Up*, no kidding, involved sanding what was appropriately called the "doughnut" of the wooden toilet seat. The mundane monotony of the job was overwhelming. Many co-workers were taking things called "black beauties" that, as one worker often said temptingly, "make you want to tap dance under water." With no desire to do Fred Astaire under water, there was little to create motivation, save one's own habits and a little goal setting: like how long it would take to sand a stack of fifty doughnuts. When a stack of doughnuts was left at the sanding station, goal-directed work commenced. As the work continued and the stack got lower and lower and the goal neared, never, never was the stack completed. Always, in the interest of smooth production, when there were just two or three doughnuts left, another stack of fifty would pile onto the waiting stack. The boring task specialization, and lack of control, were stultifying. The inability to complete a whole job was punishing. This work arrangement is close to what Charlie Chaplin parodies in *Modern Times*. Now, think of your worst and best jobs, and define the characteristics, assumptions, and practices that made them so, and design around the best of these.

Designing People Systems

The method to follow in designing the people systems is described in the Figure 8.1. Because the people systems encompass so many elements of an organization, it is easy to see the complexity and difficulty of the task, but it doesn't have to be as hard as we first imagine to design state of the art systems. What works best is to keep two things in mind that make the process simpler. First, there are often excellent people system components operating at some location or at some level of the organization that could be spread throughout the system. Second, the organization's principles offer the most direct line of thinking for developing the best systems. If we think hard about our principles, and extrapolate from them to design our people systems, the answer to the challenges of designing optimum people systems become much simpler. The most significant constraints to designing optimum people systems are these:

- We have lived in the culture so long that we have come to accept systems as they are.
- We don't think that these hallowed systems can be changed.

1. Analyze The Guiding Principles

The organizational constitution that was developed in Chapter 4 established a set of guiding principles. Those principles described the organization's principles for the ideal people environment and the principles for operational excellence. Often these principles fade into the background when people systems are being designed. The principles should be the strongest source of direction in designing effective people systems.

Steve Piersanti is recognized as a highly innovative founder of Berett-Kohler Publishers. He illustrates the point of living by and designing systems that match your principles. When asked to explain such unique practices as distributing 50% of pretax profits to "major stakeholders" — authors, employees, suppliers, and community groups — Piersanti says, "It's not a question of the benefits it brings to the company, it's a question of are you going to live your values or not? As publisher, I am not owner or lord of these literary priorities;

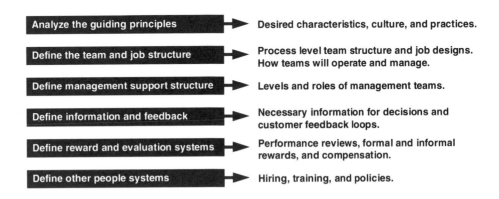

Figure 8.1 The People System Process

rather, I am trustee or steward accountable to authors, customers, employees, suppliers."

Matching principles with practices and systems is powerful. Often the degree to which the principles suggest specific systems and practices is very clear. For example, an organization may have a principle that says, "Pay for performance will drive our compensation systems." The compensation system may, however, have executive compensation that includes base pay, bonus, and stock options, middle-management pay that includes base pay and bonus, and front-line associate pay that includes base pay alone. Alignment of the principles of pay for performance with actual practices would suggest that common elements of pay systems could be applied at all levels. In another example, many organizations talk about becoming a learning organization. Does this mean that everyone receives lots of training? Not necessarily. Motorola, an advocate of learning, recently announced that every associate would receive 40 hours of training per year, every year. This level is not matched by many who profess the desire to be a learning organization. Once again, it is matching what you say you believe, with what you actually put into practice.

In addition to your own organizational principles, it helps to see what others see as some of the principles that guide the design of high performance companies. William Pasmore offers these principles for organization design.

People work better when:

- They have opportunities to satisfy personal needs through the work itself — for feedback, recognition, learning, variety, belonging to a group, moving toward a better future, autonomy, influence.

- They are involved in decisions which affect them directly.
- They are rewarded for putting forth effort and for using their judgment.
- They belong to groups which provide support, clarify values, encourage effective performance, and facilitate the accomplishment of interdependent tasks.

The Technical System (work processes) works better when:

- People are multi-skilled, understand the technology, and are aware of how their work affects the end-product.
- Problems are identified and solved at the point where they occur, by the people closest to the work.
- The technology is controlled and maintained by the people who operate it.
- Boundaries are drawn so that people are responsible for whole products or processes, instead of specific steps in the process or particular pieces of equipment.

In the book *Continuous Improvement: Teams & Tools,* the authors offered the following principles of high performance:

- **Work is best accomplished when people work together in teams.**
- **No team is an island.** No team can win without support from many other teams.
- **Every team accomplishes its work through a work process.** Every team owns part of, or all of, many work processes that produce products or services as outputs. Each team receives input from its suppliers and transforms that input into valuable output.

- **Every team can work to continuously improve the process.** Customer requirements drive the improvement process.
- **All individuals and all teams want to be winners.** Managers have the job of creating a climate where people can learn, grow, and be winners.
- **The system works just as it is designed.** People performance is a function of the system. Don't try to fix the people, fix the work system.
- **Build in quality.** People should be empowered to inspect their own quality and will rise to the level of responsibility they are given.
- **Decision-making must be at the point of attack.** Minimize bureaucracy and speed cycle times by providing the skills and knowledge required to make customer service decisions face-to-face.

Use Your Principles

You can begin this first step of people system design by looking at your guiding principles. A good beginning point is to look at each principle and attempt to extract specific corollaries and examples of that principle in action. One way of doing this is to do the following:

- Write each principle on a flipchart.
- After reading each principle, as a team ask, "Therefore we will...what?" Record the team's answers.
- Repeat asking the question two or three times and record the team's answers. Follow the guideline of working toward more specific answers at each iteration.

This process will work to show what the principles really mean. For example, a specific extension of the principle, "We will listen to our associates," could be, "Headquarters' managers will visit field offices for listening sessions quarterly." The thinking that came out of the analysis of principles should form a list of important characteristics and practices that should now be built into each of the people system components.

We have seen how our guiding principles can greatly help define what the organization's people systems should be made of. In addition, our experience is that the design of specific systems, such as feedback and evaluation, benefit from defining a set of guiding principles that are specific to this system. These system specific principles can serve as prompts for initiating ideas and criteria for evaluating the system once it has been designed. Several examples of system specific principles are included in the following sections.

2. Define The Team And Job Structure

Step 2 in designing people systems has many elements. Figure 8.2 shows the sub-steps that are required to complete this work. The approach outlined here begins with the assumption that teams of people will be the core organizational building block. There may be many types and formations of teams based on the organizing concept that you choose, but teams are most likely to be the smallest organizational unit.

Teams replace the function as the primary organizational unit in the newly designed workplace. The functional organization is not the optimum way to organize people in most cases. Teams are defined at the core work process first. This is a bottom-up approach to structure that is based on the newly defined and mapped core work processes.

The horizontal structure of teams are designed to optimize the flow of work across the organization before any support/management teams are designed. This organization turns the old functional world on its head. People from different disciplines come together in perpetual teams like those at Steelcase's corporate development center. Project-team work areas are called "neighborhoods," where designers, engineers, marketing, and purchasing people are grouped together in multi-disciplinary teams. These teams, operating a new work flow, have cut Steelcase's product development time in half.

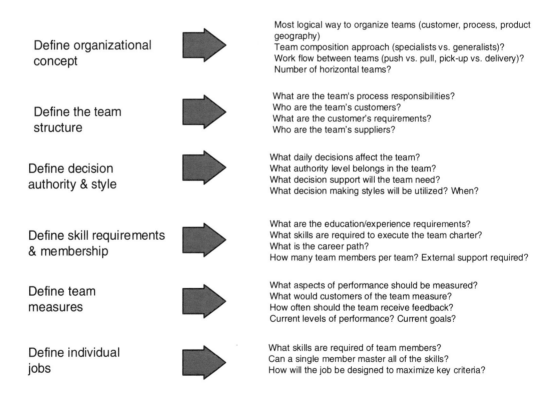

Define organizational concept	→	Most logical way to organize teams (customer, process, product geography) Team composition approach (specialists vs. generalists)? Work flow between teams (push vs. pull, pick-up vs. delivery)? Number of horizontal teams?
Define the team structure	→	What are the team's process responsibilities? Who are the team's customers? What are the customer's requirements? Who are the team's suppliers?
Define decision authority & style	→	What daily decisions affect the team? What authority level belongs in the team? What decision support will the team need? What decision making styles will be utilized? When?
Define skill requirements & membership	→	What are the education/experience requirements? What skills are required to execute the team charter? What is the career path? How many team members per team? External support required?
Define team measures	→	What aspects of performance should be measured? What would customers of the team measure? How often should the team receive feedback? Current levels of performance? Current goals?
Define individual jobs	→	What skills are required of team members? Can a single member master all of the skills? How will the job be designed to maximize key criteria?

Figure 8.2 Sub-steps for Defining Team and Job Structure

Principles For First-level Team Structure

- Have fewest possible horizontal hand-offs.
- Match structure to desired flow option, such as work cells.
- Maximum decision authority over key process choices.
- Ownership of a whole process.
- The ability to complete a final output.
- A clear internal or external customer.
- Responsibility for a measurable business result.

Types Of Teams

Perpetual teams: The idea of organizing around the team concept has been widely discussed and publicized. Despite the commonness with which teams are discussed, what we call perpetual teams are rarely a characteristic of the organization. In a true team-based organization, perpetual teams are the home base teams that operate the work processes daily. Perpetual teams should be organized around a concept other than function. They may be developed around a process, customer, product, or technology.

Virtual teams: Virtual teams are formed to assure that organizational boundaries don't harden into the same silo structures that were characteristic of the old organization. Some companies that have organized around parallel processes report that it is easy to have "process tunnels," where improvement ideas and information don't flow between identical processes. Virtual teams are employed periodically to continue to advance the reengineering thinking by sharing new ideas across the teams and assuring consistency of operation.

"As companies
reengineer, the jobs
that remain are bigger
ones that require a
higher caliber
of people."
Michael Hammer

Some of the best examples of successful virtual teams are those that respond to crisis situations. Storm response teams in power companies and crisis teams in oil or chemical companies often are the best examples of teams in action. Virtual teams may be situation driven, like a business opportunity team, or project driven, as they serve as an adjunct to the perpetual team system.

One word of caution is to be careful that a virtual team is not really doubling for an ineffective perpetual team. Some managers are proud of how well their organization has been able to take things "off-line," like the development of a new product. What is often actually occurring is that the core process and the perpetual team structure are simply not effective.

Teams do seem to be the answer to organizational fragmentation. Rarely will the team be a common functional group, rather, it will be more common to have multi-skilled teams that own whole processes or customers. As Paul A. Allaire described "rugged groupism" in *At Work*: "*We are coming to believe in the value of bringing things together to create work units or teams responsible for a whole set of activities. This concept, of course, rests on faith in the human spirit and intellect. It assumes that a diverse group of people — using their own creativity, innovation, judgement, intuition, and brainpower — can do a better job in today's world of constant change than any set of 'formal procedures,' methods, or controls administered by a remote, centralized management.*"

After a team is defined, the grid in Figure 8.3 can help to assure that the responsibilities and supporting relationships are clearly established.

Job Design

There are many arguments about what a job should be. Some common wisdom says that people should have the job they do best. We often sound like Ford and his penchant for specialists. Robert Heinlein, writing in *The Notebooks of Lazarus Long* has another view: "A human being should be able to change a diaper, plan an invasion, butcher a hog, conn a ship, design a building, write a sonnet, balance accounts, build a wall, set a bone, comfort the dying, take orders, give orders, cooperate, act alone, solve equations, analyze a new

	Operating Team	First Level Support	Second Level Support
1. What is the primary purpose of this team?			
2. What does this team do that no other team can?			
3. What results does this team assure will be accomplished?			
4. What wouldn't be accomplished without this team?			
5. How will this team measure process performance and results?			
6. What are the key decisions this team will make?			

Figure 8.3 Team Responsibilities Chart

problem, pitch manure, program a computer, cook a tasty meal, fight efficiently, die gallantly. Specialization is for insects."

Principles Of Job Design

The team's work must be broken down into chunks we conveniently call jobs. The individual responsibilities of the team member may be defined by the reengineering team or they may be left for the team to determine for themselves. The general principles of good job design suggest the following:

- Pay, security, benefits, safety, health, due process
- Learning
- Decision-making
- Social support
- Work that provides meaning and dignity
- Desirable future
- Variety
- Challenge
- Autonomy and discretion
- Integrity of tasks
- Physical or electronic proximity to teammates
- Opportunity for growth of skills or increase levels of mastery

In defining teams and jobs it is generally best when both are generalists. When this is not possible, teams of specialists should have general responsibilities. To own a whole process a team must be comprised of multi-skilled members, or it must be made up of specialists who work together to assure smooth hand-offs of work. In many cases we know the level of technical expertise for a given job, say heart surgery, requires a high level of specialized knowledge and skill. Heart surgeons should do heart surgery all day and not dabble in brain surgery, or an occasional gall bladder. The total team in the operating room, however, is comprised the heart surgeon, surgical nurses, anesthesiologists, and other specialists. The patient counts on the team to work seamlessly and flawlessly to assure the desired outcome. Each team member is a specialist, but the key operating team is a cohesive unit. Even when high specialization is required, there is frequently a team construction that puts the specialists together to accomplish work.

Decision-Making Authority And Support

One of the most popular words today is empowerment. We are urged to empower and we are cautioned against the anarchy it may create. Empowerment is basically a simple idea. We look for an answer to the question: Which decisions can intelligent, responsible human beings make about their daily work? In order to empower, one must first accept that there is no such thing as perfect decision-making. Even the smartest executives sometimes make dumb decisions. Nevertheless, front-line teams can make wise and reasoned decisions when they have information, skills and responsibility. However, asking a team to make decisions without these three elements is like asking someone to fly a plane with some of the dials blacked out.

A corollary of empowerment is the idea of responsibility. Responsibility goes beyond the idea of accountability. Responsibility is a level of maturity and ownership, while accountability often refers to a parent-child relationship where someone will be handing out consequences. We have come to believe that the highest form of ownership is a state of being, not a state of holding; it's about "being responsible" not holding someone else accountable.

To operationalize responsibility is to assign specific decision-making responsibility. The exercise below describes how decision authority can be defined, beginning with the levels of responsibility that is desired for the first level perpetual team.

1. List the key organizational decisions on 3 x 5 cards.
2. List the key process decisions on 3 x 5 cards.
3. Begin dealing the cards and assigning them to the level one team.
4. Continue to assign until you run out of them.
5. Next, assign decisions in the same manner to the first level management support team.
6. When you have run out of cards, you have a clue about the number of management levels that will be required.

3. Define Management Support Structure

What kind of support will the operating team require in order to operate its processes? Using the decision assignment as a model, begin building support levels following these principles.

Principles Of Management Support

• Fewest number of layers
• Accomplish unique work that supports front line teams
• Adds unique value
• Not an information-passer because everyone has all of the information

- Spans of control greater than 1/6 and as high as 1/20

4. Define Information And Feedback Systems

For a team to operate effectively and make the kinds of decisions that are envisioned, information must be provided. Team performance information and customer feedback are the two categories of information being considered here. Principles to guide this development could include those provided here.

Principles For Information And Feedback
- Everyone in the organization receives regular customer feedback.
- Information is available and easily accessible.
- Internal customer feedback is face-to-face.
- Individual and team feedback is simple, frequent, and development-oriented.
- Feedback is always 360 degrees.

5. Define Reward And Evaluation Systems

Reward and evaluation are central features of a high motivation and learning environment. In a recent case, a group from a human resources department mapped the performance evaluation process at their company. One could easily see upon examining the process map that the primary purpose of the process was to assure that a raise higher than tolerable would not be given. There were six sign-off points whose purpose was only to check the amount of the raise. The feedback and learning opportunities were not checked, but the raise amount was checked an absurd number of times. The real purpose of the process was to keep too much money from going out, not to assure that good

learning was going on in the person. We design processes to maximize what
we really think is important.

The most effective pay systems are often based on ability and results.
What a team accomplishes and what it has the capability to do should matter
most in compensation. The days of regular raises are over in this period of
price and profit compression. Coopers & Lybrand report that a third of the 184
companies surveyed plan to implement pay-for-performance plans in 1994, up
from 24 percent last year. Merit increases will continue to decline. The most
common type of performance-based pay is team or group incentive.

Similarly, many companies are tying the compensation of employees to
stock options. This is an effective way of connecting employees to the authentic consequences of the external environment.

Team-based compensation: Team-based pay is a direct match with
many organizational principles that say that everyone wins or loses as a team.
These systems buck a long held tradition of individual compensation based on
individual contribution. Brian Joiner illustrates the benefits of team-based
compensation and evaluation by describing what would happen to a rowing
crew if they were are scored individually following normal curve thinking. Very
few A's, a few B's and C's and probably at least one F. If the individuals work
to excel individually the scull goes erratically. What makes the system work is
when everyone strokes according to a common pace.

Principles that may guide the design of this reward and evaluation systems include:

Principles Of Reward And Evaluation

- Everyone wants to be, and is able to be, a winner.
- Rewards will be intangible and tangible.
- Evaluations will be based on 360 feedback.
- Compensation will be balanced between individual, team, and organizational performance.
- Formal annual written appraisals do not add value.
- Giving feedback is an important responsibility.
- Everyone can be a superstar. Normal curves need not apply.
- The evaluation process should be about developmental feedback, not raises.
- Feedback will flow in all directions and be valued equally.

Examples of innovative people systems include:

- Corning has the objective of having gainsharing at all of its plants.
- Lincoln Electric is well documented as the company where employees' year-end bonuses average 97% of their regular base pay. The company has gone 54 years without a losing quarter.
- ITT Financial uses a program called PAC that links employees to 65 P&L statements. Home office employees are linked to a combined P&L.
- At Nucor Steel, 10% of pre-tax earnings are distributed to all employees.
- Federal Express has a system of spot rewards where any manager

can give an associate an award on the spot of $100 for excellent service and effort.

6. Define Other Support Systems

Other systems that may require a special design effort could include the following:

- Training
- Hiring
- Policies

A thought to keep in mind throughout the design of people systems is to remember that it is almost woven into our fabric to design systems to the lowest common denominator. If a computer was stolen once, a new policy is inflicted upon thousands of people who are completely trustworthy. We misjudge the erosion of commitment and motivation that comes from systems that are designed to keep some from sinking to the floor. The reality is that these approaches keep many more from reaching for the stars.

9 Implementing And Managing Change

9

The Phases Of Change

A Model For Change

Guidelines For Leading Change

Implementing Reengineered Processes And Systems

Implementing And Managing Change

The reengineering work has been completed and now it is time to take the paper plans and begin to turn them into reality. The major tasks at this time are to be sure you have a great appreciation for change and to make wise choices about the pace and scope for implementation of new processes and systems.

Before making the key implementation decisions about the scope and pace of implementation, it is first important to understand the dynamics of change and the keys to leading effective change. The next two sections will address these two topics of change.

The Phases Of Change

Change is one of those things that everyone talks about but most of the talk isn't very helpful. People say, "Get ready for change." But they say it like they say, "Get ready for that big wave," at the beach — you know you're going to get knocked over but you might as well brace yourself. Heads up! Good luck! I hope it works out. Do your best. Hold your breath.

Perhaps the simplest and most profound description of personal change is provided by William Bridges in *Transitions: Making Sense of Life's Change*, who described three phases of change: endings, confusion and distress, and new beginnings. These three phases hearken back to historian Arnold J. Toynbee's observation in *A Study of History* that stated each civilization has encountered a time of trouble and disintegration, followed by a time of with-drawal and return, and finally a time of new energy and direction. Toynbee notes that this basic pattern has applied to ancient as well as modern civiliza-tions, advanced as well as simple, eastern as well as western. Noel Tichy and Stratford Sherman, in *Control Your Destiny or Someone Else Will*, have described Bridges' three phases in the context of a larger model for organiza-tional change being used at General Electric. In the GE model, organizational change happens in three acts. In the first act "Awakening," the organization's confrontation of its need for transformation corresponds to and interacts with individuals' struggles with related personal endings. The need to change and resistance to change are evident. In the second act "Envisioning," the organiza-tion creates a motivating vision and mobilizes commitment. Individuals are in a transition period. The new vision provides individuals with a perspective on both endings and new beginnings. In the third act "Rearchitecturing," the organization builds a new social architecture. Correspondingly, individuals embark on new beginnings and learn new scripts for successful behavior.

Endings

Bridges notes that every transition begins with an ending. Those who initiate change may tend to minimize the importance of ending the old way, as if that would be admitting that the change was a mistake. On the other hand, those who go into change unwillingly may find it hard to admit that a new beginning is at hand — they mournfully focus on the ending of the old way. Those forced to change may even be emotionally invested in seeing no good come of the change. The key point is that we have to say good-bye to and mourn the old way, even if the new way is something we want.

"Change is not made without inconvenience, even from worse to better."

Richard Hooker,

English theologian

The concept of endings explains a lot. You may wonder why people complain even when they get the change they want: "I wish I could have more control over my work — Hey, who's going to tell me what to do?" It's because *we tend to identify ourselves with the circumstances of our lives.* That's the rest of that maxim: "Be careful what you wish for you just might get it...then you'll have to say good-bye to something familiar that you identify as a part of *you* and adjust to something unfamiliar that's not yet a part of *you.*" (O.K., the whole maxim is not as catchy.)

The concept of endings also explains why *people generally like to change but they do not like to be changed.* A person who is initiating a change is often prepared to say good-bye to the old way (or already has) and is prepared to embrace a new way of his or her choosing. That person may have already envisioned a new self, one that is connected to the new way. If a person is forced into a change, then he or she must define a new self on someone else's timetable.

Bridges notes that there are several stages within an ending:

Disengagement
In this phase of the ending we are separated from the familiar, thus deprived of familiar ways of knowing ourselves. For example, the loved one is gone or the job no longer exists.

Disidentification
Most people at some point during a change feel that they are not quite

sure who they are anymore. In this phase of the ending, we have to give up former ways of defining ourselves. For example, a recent college graduate in her first full-time job can no longer think of herself as "a college student."

Disenchantment

During this phase of the ending we have to realize that a big part of our old reality was in our heads, not in the situation. The "enchantment" that we held for the previous situation was what we longed for: the flawless, ideal relationship, job, neighborhood, or whatever. To make a successful change, we have to become disenchanted with the old way, but not disillusioned. Disillusioned people reject the earlier case but keep the old enchanted view of, for example, a job or romantic relationship, staying on a perpetual quest for the perfect one and always being disappointed.

Disorientation

In this phase of the ending we lose our sense of direction. We tend to lose interest in old goals and plans. Things that used to be important don't seem so important now. In an ending, we are torn between the desire to keep going and growing, and the impulse to stay and repeat. It is important to let ourselves and others react to endings. *Endings are ordeals because they challenge our sense of who we are.*

The Neutral Zone

After the ending phase, we experience a vague, fuzzy time that Bridges calls "the neutral zone." This phase is a period of confusion and stress because there is a gap in continuity between the old and new. There is a great feeling of

*"The basic fact of
today is the
tremendous pace
of change
in human life."
Jawaharlal Nehru,
Indian statesman*

emptiness during this phase, but the neutral zone is important because it is only from the perspective of the old way that the new way looks frightening. From any other perspective, it just looks like another chapter of life. In other words, the new job looks intimidating because it's new to *you* — but to everyone else, it's just work!

In the neutral zone we have to take the opportunity to discover what we really want. We have to think of what would be unlived if life just stopped and we didn't begin anew.

Beginning Anew

In this final phase we must embrace the new. We have to stop getting ready and *act*. We have to identify ourselves with the final result of the new beginning. What is it going to feel like when we've actually done whatever it is that we're setting out to do? As Bridges points out, "We have to take things step by step and resist the siren song that tells of some other route where everything is exciting and meaningful."

The third concept that is essential during change is habit formation, that is, how we learn and how we teach ourselves new routines. As human beings, we learn to act in certain ways under certain circumstances to be successful. When we are successful on some regular basis, our actions become habits and we act competently on a routine basis. When the circumstances change or when our actions are not successful anymore, we may continue fruitlessly, trying the same action harder or we may simply stop altogether. Obviously, neither of these responses is effective for becoming successful. Instead, we need to learn new ways of acting that can succeed in the new circumstances. We may learn by trial-and-error, by observation, or through someone's coaching.

When we do, our new actions may not be successful at first because we are still learning them. In this case, we need to encounter some shorter-term sense of success, usually in the form of recognition from others, so that we don't return to the old habits or give up. The basics of learning are important here: the more frequent and immediate the recognition from others, the stronger our new ways of acting become. Short-term targets and small improvement steps make this easier. Feedback on our behavior and opportunities to practice are essential.

A Model For Change

How should a change agent think about change? Figure 9.1 shows a simple but powerful model for change that has strong implications for the role of the change agent.

Our experience of change occurs in four stages: Awareness, Understanding, Implementation, and Change. In the Awareness stage, we must discover why the change is important. In the Understanding stage, we must learn the concepts and skills we need to change successfully. In the Implementation stage, we put the learning into practice and try the new way. In the final Change stage, the change becomes permanent because the new environment (or systems that we have created) support and reward our new habits.

"Future shock... the
shattering stress and
disorientation that we
induce in individuals
by subjecting them to
too much change in
too short a time."
Alvin Toffler,
author

Don't be mislead by the simplicity of the model. The need for all four of the stages is profound. Can you think of times when training happened but people didn't understand why it was needed? Can you think of times when training happened, but the training was never put into practice? Can you think of times when associates of the organization followed a new program because staffers emphasized it, but it never stuck? The model explains many simple truths about change that have been discovered through painful experience in unsuccessful change efforts.

The Awareness Stage

In the Awareness stage, we ask, "What's going on? Why should I change? What was wrong with the old way?" We may be excited about the new way, but more likely we feel anxious, defensive, and suspicious. Our self-image is connected to the old way. Human nature and common sense tell us not to throw away familiar routines unnecessarily. Strength of habit keeps us in the old way. Our thoughts might turn to imagined problems with the new way. To change, we must understand the disadvantages of staying with the old way and the benefits of the new way.

We often don't listen to the first calls for change. Sometimes it takes repeated messages. Some of us don't start flossing the first time the dentist mentions it. Some of us don't start saving more the first time we read an article about personal finance. Some companies don't change as fast as they should, nor do some people within a company change as fast as they could. A rule of thumb for change agents is "7 x 7." A change agent should communicate about a change and why it is important seven times in seven different ways. If you are trying to create awareness about a change in your organization, you might try 1) a guest speaker, 2) a memo, 3) a video, 4) a breakfast meeting, 5) a voice-mail message, 6) banners, and 7) a letter to associates' homes.

The Understanding Stage

In the Understanding stage, we ask, "What do I have to know? How do I do this?" This is the learning stage. Once we become truly aware of the need to change, we are filled with questions. We absorb information about the new way and we begin to practice new skills. Training is the order of the day. Although essential, it is important to note that the typical training class can be

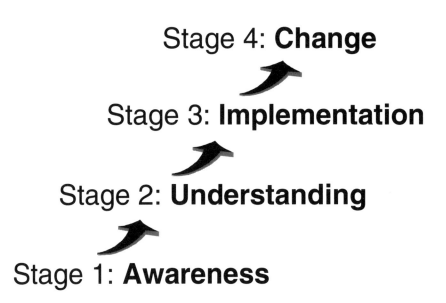

Figure 9.1 The Stages of Change

an inefficient method of transferring information and competence. In a classic article, Kulik, Jaksa, and Kulik identified the components of effective individualized instruction. The components are: a) a high mastery standard, b) frequent quizzing, c) immediate feedback, and d) regular review. Unfortunately, these components are difficult to build into adult training. For adults, training must be interesting, relevant, and dignified. Adults learn from stories, pertinent examples, and if possible, through experiences. A mastery requirement and frequent quizzing can be jarring in adult training situations. This is to say that the change agent must make sure that understanding is really occurring when training is provided.

The Implementation Stage

In the Implementation stage, we must put our new understanding into practice. Often missteps and mistakes occur; support is needed. A truism of training is that, without follow-up, participants usually remember only about 15% of training content and only act on about 15% of that. Though this is shocking at first, if we consider it, it is logical. While participants are in training, their work piles up and the first few days afterward are spent catching up, doing things the way they did them before, only faster. In the meantime, they are gradually forgetting the information and skills they learned. If and when they finally put their learning into practice, they are bound to encounter problems. The real world is a harsh teacher and the learners will probably not be competent at first. Without perceptive coaching and kind words, most participants are likely to return to their pre-training habits.

Thus, implementation by the learner and, if possible, follow-up by a coach are essential for change. The coach may serve as an observer, feedback provider, sounding board, advisor, reviewer of training, and source of encouragement.

The Change Stage

In the Change stage, systems must be put in place to maintain the new way. A permanent change cannot take place if the environment is set up to be counter to the new behaviors. The new habits must be successful in the environment if they are to maintain. Otherwise, change makes the person a cultural deviant.

Guidelines for Leading Change

Leaders must provide true leadership for large-scale organization change to be successful. Leading change effectively is one of the important jobs of leaders in a world that knows change as its only constant.

To lead change you have to change. If the organization is nothing more, or less, than a collection of individuals, then organizational transformation is born of personal transformation. Organizational transformation is accompanied by, and caused by, personal transformation. No personal transformation is more important than that of the leaders. The ten points that follow are intended to help leaders think about what will be required if they are to negotiate the tortuous road of change successfully.

1. Fire in the belly. Don't put your organization through a profound change unless you have steeled yourself for the effort and have a passionate conviction about the necessity for, and value of, change. Think about what the organization will need to be like five and ten years from now to be successful. Your vision must reflect passion and urgency for change. It must describe a future that has benefits strong enough to pull an organization through the tough work to come. Your task is to create a compelling case for action in your own mind before going further. Don't risk your organization or cause the pain of changing to be part of a fad.

2. Honest self-assessment. Vaughn Beals of Harley-Davidson noted that all of their efforts to revitalize Harley were unsuccessful until the leaders said, "The problem is us." To lead change, you must see yourself as you are seen by the followers in your organization. The trouble is that leaders are usually the last people in the organization to hear honest feedback. If you don't know how the leadership team is perceived, find out. Conduct a survey to feel the pulse of the people and learn how the organization as a whole, and the leadership team in particular, are viewed.

3. Balance time and priorities. Leaders signal the importance of initiatives by how they spend their time. The problem is that there are too many ways to spend leadership time that are all "right." No one will challenge how leaders spend their time, so the senior team must establish the strategic priority of the quality initiative and define how each member of the team will spend time to support the effort. Some general suggestions about how to spend time are:

- Spend at least one quarter of your time with customers.
- Spend at least one quarter of your time with people at least two levels

removed from your team. This should include significant time with frontline
employees who deal with customers every day.

- Spend more time listening to the organization than communicating your
  message about the direction and performance goals of the company.

- Spend 10% of your time learning the skills and tools of continuous
  improvement.

- Demonstrate through your actions that the surest way to see immediate
  improvement and long term results is through the application of continuous improvement practices.

4. Model the principles. The tools of quality and continuous improvement are straightforward and can be mastered from the shop floor to the
executive tower. The tools have their greatest value when they are applied in
an environment that has adopted a new paradigm for managing. Guiding
principles articulate this new paradigm and leaders have the job of making the
new paradigm real. Principles are the rock-solid tenets that all employees can
count on. They offer security and confidence by making leadership behavior
predictable. Demonstrate the validity of the principles, when they are developed, by showing how they guide the tough decisions.

5. Incorporate within your strategic framework. A quality or
continuous improvement effort should be part of the overall strategic plan for
the organization. This plan must be integrated into the fabric of the organization
and must be real for associates at every level. The best way to make it real is
to mainstream the process into the planning and objective-setting process.

6. Understand the dynamics of change. Figure 9.2 describes the important dynamics of change. Leaders must be aware of the learning curves, intellectual and habitual, and the accompanying emotional stages the people of your organization will experience.

The curve of intellectual knowledge occurs as a result of training and moves up the change axis quickly. The habit change curve moves up the change axis much more slowly. The distance between what has been learned intellectually and what is practiced habitually represents the change gap. Everyone has probably experienced the discomfort that this gap brings. In tennis, for instance, one can be an intellectual champion commenting expertly on every situation and shot, while being unable to execute any of the shots on the court. Change is successful when ideas and information have been translated into enduring habits.

There are very predictable emotional stages that accompany learning and change (see Figure 9.2). Change always initiates excitement or fear at the outset. We have all experienced the combined emotions of elation, "Great, I got the job," followed by fear, "Oh no, how am I going to do that job?"

The second stage of change is the most difficult. At the point when learning is greatest, the learner has also become painfully aware of the gap between what is in the book and what is in the habits. Many feel doubt and even disillusionment at this point. This is like week two of a diet: you know what has to be done and you also know just how hard it will be to reach the goal. This is a stage that must be traversed because awareness of the gap between what you want, and where you are, is the catalyst for fundamental change.

In the final stage, positive emotions accompany the rapidly growing habit curve. This is the fun and easy part of change. New skills are working and broad applications are being discovered.

Every individual and every team will go through the curve at a different pace. People will be at different stages throughout the change effort. Those who have confidence in their use of new skills and ideas will often be intolerant

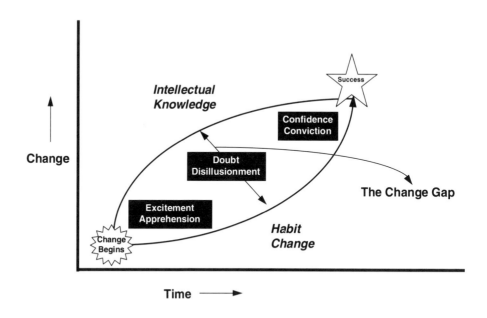

Figure 9.2 Intellectual and Habit Curves

of those who are working through periods of doubt. Helpful leadership will provide empathy, coaching, and reward for effort during this stage.

7. Expect cynicism. Expect cynicism from employees who have been through one too many programs. Cynicism should be anticipated, understood, and used as a source of energy for change. Cynicism comes from cognitive dissonance. Cognitive dissonance describes how we feel when there is imbalance between our stated beliefs and our daily behavior. Individuals seek balance by changing behavior or rationalizing beliefs. Dissonance can be a constructive force for change in an organization when individuals are empowered to help bring about positive change. The practical lessons are:

- Enlist everyone in the change process. Change shouldn't be something that is happening to anyone, but rather, change is a process being brought about by the people of the organization.
- Leaders must reduce unnecessary dissonance by behaving consistently with the vision, mission, and principles.

8. Plan to win with results. The plan to change the culture of an organization must be well thought out and comprehensive. Develop a plan that is designed to win by articulating the results that should be achieved as the process is implemented. Set improvement goals in the soft category (cultural characteristics) and the hard category (business performance).

A macro plan is essential at the outset, but don't "fall in love" with the plan. Fall in love with the vision and mission, and modify the plan as you learn and as events change. Stay constant about where you are going, and stay flexible about how to get there.

Don't wait for the perfect plan or the perfect time before you begin. Neither has ever existed. Begin with a three-year macro plan that defines the future state and three or four transition states that the organization will move through on its progression toward your vision. Develop detailed training and implementation plans that have a planning horizon of 90 to 180 days. Continue developing these 180-day plans incorporating the learning you have gained.

9. Stay externally focused on the customer. Change efforts of this kind often fail because the link between the effort and the purpose of the business is not clear from the outset or becomes vague. Should this linkage deteriorate, the first crisis will push the plan onto the back shelf. Maintain the importance of the effort by staying externally focused and constantly linking the effort to the ultimate customer satisfaction goals of the enterprise. Stay customer-focused by:

- Establishing customer satisfaction and retention as the most important measure of the company.
- Saturating the organization with the voice of the customer.
- Sharing all customer survey data with everyone.
- Copying others on customer feedback.
- Meeting "belly-to-belly" with real customers informally and frequently and sharing observations.

10. Savor the quest. Your vision and principles will make this odyssey a noble quest. As you embark on this voyage, it helps to embrace the philosophy of continuous improvement from the outset and begin to derive satisfaction from the fact that the journey has begun. Each step of progress, each moment of learning from every mistake, can be a source of satisfaction and motivation to continue.

Implementing Reengineered Processes And Systems

The first task of implementation is to review the recommendations that are proposed by the design team. Design team recommendations can be sorted into four categories. These categories are:

- Accept for immediate implementation.
- Accept for phased-in implementation.
- Accept with further detail design required.
- Reject.

The second task is to decide on the pace and scope of the implementation plan. To think about this decision, there are three steps suggested. The first is to answer these questions.

- What is the urgency for implementation?
- What is the resource requirement of implementation?
- What is the organization's tolerance for implementation?

The second step is to review the business case for action, and the third step is to review the vision, mission, and principles.

Once recommendations have been categorized and the major sources of input have been considered, the steering team should have a strong sense of what should be implemented immediately and what should be put on the back burner. With these choices made, preparation can begin for implementation.

Generally, new process designs and new team configurations should be implemented simultaneously, so preparation must be in the form of process operation and technical training, and organizational and team skills training. Most reengineering failures are the result of inadequate preparation. People are formed into teams without the skills to operate as team members and team leaders without learning the skills required to be a team. New processes are designed on paper, but process operators are not trained in the steps or the technology of the process.

People systems typically fit into the category requiring further design. Generally these new systems, like team pay or 360-degree feedback, should be implemented within six months of when new processes and new team structures have been implemented. Figure 9.3 offers a generic Gantt chart of an implementation timeline.

Implementation requires constant review, evaluation, and adjustment. The steering team should take over from the design team as the champion of the recommendations, and must manage the implementation as it would any strategically-significant project.

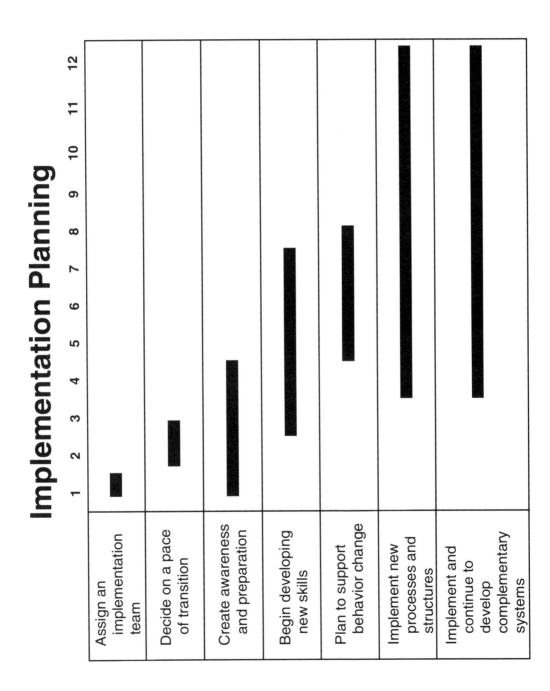

Figure 9.3 Implementation Planning Gantt Chart

10

Reengineering Toolbox

10

State-Change Analysis

Critical Value-Added Diagram

Process Prioritization And Analysis

Combined Macro Map And Relationship Map

Process Steps And Customer Requirements

Envisioning A New Culture

Pie In The Sky

Reengineering Toolbox

This chapter offers an extended tool kit for the reengineering team. Several tools will be described in this chapter that will allow the team to look at work from a new perspective and generate fresh thinking.

The first section of the chapter presents tools for process reengineering and redesign. The second section offers methods that will be helpful in defining ideal people systems.

The final few pages of the chapter include a glossary of process thinking terms and a reengineering simulation exercise. The *Pie In The Sky Pizza Company* case can be used to practice the skills and apply the tools of reengineering.

Feel free to copy the tools and the case for your use.

#1. State-Change Analysis

When to use:

This tool is especially helpful when the team is trying to analyze the process without remaining rooted in the activities that are involved in the process today. The state-change method is designed to look at the important transformations that must happen to input as it goes through a process. The state changes can then be compared to the process steps today to spot those steps that do not contribute directly to the essential state change.

How to construct:

1. Begin by defining the state changes using the From/To construction.
2. Focus only on what happens to the input in terms of transformations.
3. List the process steps on a parallel line above the state changes.
4. Draw arrows from the current activities to the state changes that the step helps to accomplish.

Advantages:

This method lets you define the minimum state changes and then evaluate the importance of process steps based on which ones actually help accomplish the state change. A second benefit is that you may decide that some of the interim state changes can be eliminated. For example, in our baking a cake example, we may decide that we can mix the ingredients in the same pan they will be baked in, and a necessary transformation goes away. More directly, we can work to eliminate steps that do not contribute to the state changes.

Process: Baking a Cake

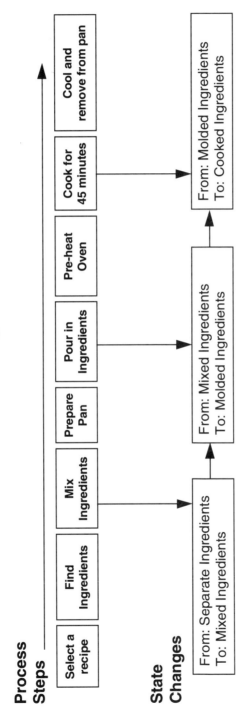

Process Steps

| Select a recipe | Find Ingredients | Mix Ingredients | Prepare Pan | Pour in Ingredients | Pre-heat Oven | Cook for 45 minutes | Cool and remove from pan |

State Changes

From: Separate Ingredients
To: Mixed Ingredients

From: Mixed Ingredients
To: Molded Ingredients

From: Molded Ingredients
To: Cooked Ingredients

Tool #1 State-change Analysis

#2. Critical Value-added Diagram

When to use:

Use the diagram to analyze the sub-steps in a process and isolate which sub-steps add the most value at each sub-step.

How to construct:

1. Begin with the macro process map.
2. On a separate page, list the key activities in sequence that occur at each macro step.
3. Draw the stair-step bars and list each sub-activity for each macro step.
4. Indicate with a star or red flag the key sub-steps within each macro step where the highest value-adding is created. These key steps are the ones that assure that the output from the macro step will be sufficient to begin the next macro step.

Advantages:

This tool will allow you to accomplish two things. First, it lets you develop a process map at a high level, and it also helps you map the detailed sub-steps within the process. Second, it lets you define the critical value-adding sub-steps so that you can decide how to eliminate or simplify other sub-steps that may not add value and focus on designing the process to maximize the value-adding steps.

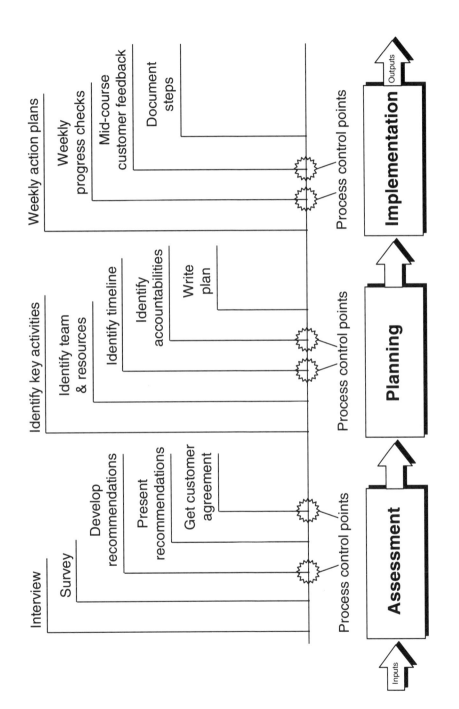

Tool #2 Critical Value-added Diagram

#3. Process Prioritization And Analysis

When to use:

When selecting a major process to redesign or reengineer, this tool provides a high-level scan of the capability of each process. It lets you compare the processes in terms of how they contribute to organizational success.

How to construct:

1. Define the critical success factors for the organization. Answer the question, "Our future success depends on our ability to_____?"
2. Discuss and agree on the success factors and list them across the top of the matrix.
3. List the organization's core processes down the left side.
4. Rate each process in terms of its contribution to fulfilling the critical success factors. The contribution of the process is rated from 1 to 5, with the highest number meaning the greatest contribution.
5. Rate the process in terms of its overall performance. The grade is subjective, but should be based on an agreed upon set of criteria.
6. Accumulate the points for the success factors and put this in the point total column. Multiply the point total times the number equivalent for the grade. The higher the final score, the greater the need for significant process improvement.

Advantages:

This is a thorough way of evaluating all core processes.

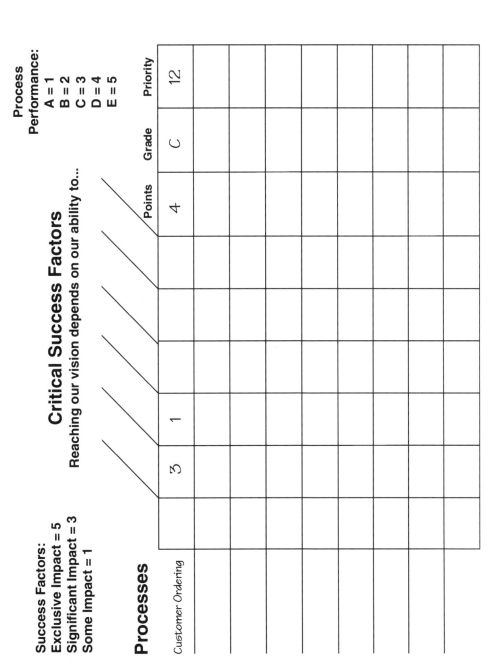

Success Factors:
Exclusive Impact = 5
Significant Impact = 3
Some Impact = 1

Critical Success Factors

Reaching our vision depends on our ability to...

Process
Performance:
A = 1
B = 2
C = 3
D = 4
E = 5

Processes

Processes							Points	Grade	Priority
Customer Ordering	3	1					4	C	12

Tool #3 Process Prioritization and Analysis

#4. Combined Macro Map And Relationship Map

When to use:

Use this combination mapping method when you have developed a high-level macro map, but decide that you need more detail either for analytical purposes, or for another group to understand in order to implement it.

How to construct:

1. Draw the standard macro map as illustrated in the example.
2. Use the macro blocks as the category labels going down the left axis of the relationship map.
3. Across from each macro step begin defining the sub-steps.
4. Use the flowcharting symbols to further define decisions and flows between categories of activity.

Advantages:

By taking the macro steps and using these steps as the categories for the relationship map, we can develop additional detail without identifying groups or people who will operate the steps. We are able to stay purely focused on the process and not get into the people-ownership issues before the process has been completely mapped out.

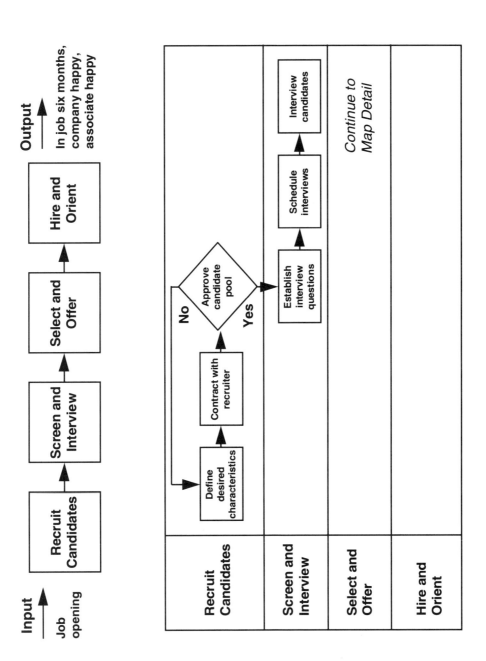

Tool #4 Combined Macro Map and Relationship Map

#5. Process Definition Tool

When to use:

Use this tool during the process definition and customer requirements steps of process redesign, or at the initial step in reengineering when the output is redefined.

How to construct:

1. Identify the process in the macro block.
2. Describe the input that begins the process and the output.
3. Identify the customer of the process and list their requirements.
4. Identify the supplier to the process and list the input requirements.

Advantages:

This approach is a very clean way of assuring good process definition, process boundary identification, and customer and supplier requirements. It is a "must" first step in process redesign.

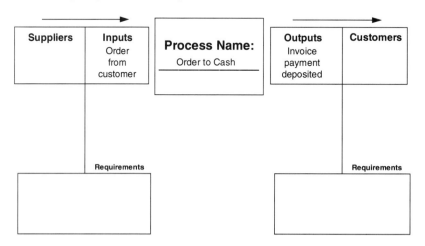

Tool #5 Process Definition Tool

#6. Mapping Symbols

In any process map it is helpful to have an array of symbols to use to depict as much detail of the process flow as you find useful for analysis, or for teaching about the construction of a new process. The classic process mapping symbols are shown below.

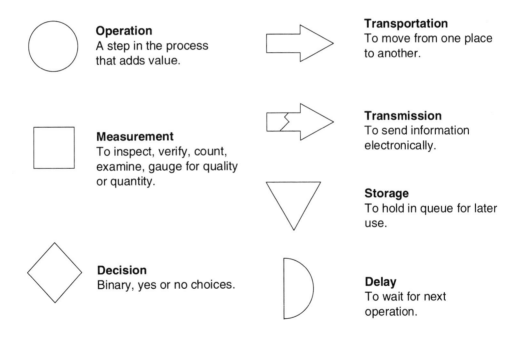

Operation
A step in the process that adds value.

Transportation
To move from one place to another.

Measurement
To inspect, verify, count, examine, gauge for quality or quantity.

Transmission
To send information electronically.

Storage
To hold in queue for later use.

Decision
Binary, yes or no choices.

Delay
To wait for next operation.

Tool #6 Mapping Symbols

#7. Process Steps Correlated With Requirements

When to use:

When you want to look at the steps in a process from the perspective of the customer or when you want to be sure that the focus of your effort is on the steps that matter most in meeting customer requirements, use this technique.

How to construct:

1. List the major steps in the process across the top of the matrix.
2. List the key customer requirements down the left column.
3. For each requirement, work across to the right and check the relationship of the step to the requirement.
4. Rate the step's relationship to the requirement as highly correlated, somewhat correlated, or negatively correlated.
5. Sum the horizontal rows and arrive at either positive or negative numbers.

Advantages:

This tool highlights the steps that are not related to the requirements and, even more significantly, the steps that are negatively correlated with the requirements. The negatively correlated steps should be eliminated. There may be ample justification for the step based on internal needs, but there is no justification for the step based on what matters most.

Process: Insurance Claim

High Correlation = 3

Medium Correlation = 1

Inverse Correlation = -3

Customer Requirements	Sort & Input	Validate	Check Deductible	Approve Payment	Issue Payment	Total Points
Fast	➡	➡	➡	➡	⬅	-9
Accurate			⬆	⬆	⬅	+5
Consistent with Policy			⬅		⬅	+6

Tool #7 Process Steps Correlated with Requirements

#8. Envisioning A New Culture

Imagine making a visit to Microsoft in Redmond, Washington. You might notice the following:

- Bill Gates wears polo shirts and no ties.
- There are few offices, instead mostly work centers and cubicles.
- People decorate their work spaces with wild pictures etc.
- The place reminds you more of a college than a company.
- People come and go at widely variable times with no 9:00 and 5:00 rush in and out.
- Intense debates are happening in hallways, over lunch, as people are walking to meetings.
- People look a little tired, worn down, but driven.
- There seems to be immense enthusiasm about work.

What single word descriptors come to mind as you leave:

-
-
-

The descriptors should be easy to arrive at. To begin seeing your organization through outside eyes, and also to start to picture the organization of the future, do the same exercise on your company.

Imagine the a new visitor comes to your company for a similar tour.

What observations would the person make?

-
-
-

What single words might they use at the end of a day to vividly describe your company?

-
-
-

Imagine it is two years from now. What observations do you hope a new visitor would make?

-
-
-
-
-
-
-

#9. Identify Desirable Cultural Traits

Culture refers to characteristics that can be considered on a continuum of extremes. Some of the extremes are listed below. As an exercise, select the desired future traits of your company and then describe what people systems would require change in order to make this trait common in the culture.

Formal	Casual
Risk-taking	Careful
Authoritarian	Participative
Proactive	Reactive
Fact based	Opinion based
Rule governed	Principle driven
Open	Closed
What makes sense	Protocol
Rank and privilege	Egalitarian
Paper based	People based
Old boyish	Performance based
Protective	Expansive
Autocracy	Meritocracy
High control	Low control
Look good	Do good
External focus	Internal focus

Tool #9 Identifying Desirable Cultural Traits

The Pie In The Sky Pizza Company:
A Reengineering Case

The Situation:

You are a member of an organizational design team, physically and mentally tired, who ends up on a plane next to a gregarious pizza shop owner from suburban New Jersey named Carmine. A rotund man in his late 60s, Carmine is returning from a singles vacation in the Caribbean. Against your will, Carmine engages you in conversation about small businesses, entrepreneurialism, and general economic survival. You trade business cards and leave the plane even more exhausted and groggy than before.

Two months later you receive a registered letter at work from a law firm and are shocked to discover 1) that Carmine has passed away at a Meet-Your-Bahama-Mama Party in Atlantic City, and 2) that Carmine has left his pizza shop, The Pie in the Sky Pizza Company, to you! His will states that you showed so much sensitivity to the issues of today's business owner that he felt that you should have an opportunity to put your ideas into practice for your own gain. (Carmine's lawyer intimates that leaving the shop to you also allowed Carmine to send a final message to his lazy cousin Rocco in Bayonne who expected to inherit it.)

During your first few days at your new place of business, you soak up information like a true organizational designer. Pie in the Sky has not grown in the five years that it has been in existence. The shop experiences one or two customer complaints per day (usually about cold pizzas), which is generally

The Pie in the Sky Pizza Company (floor plan)

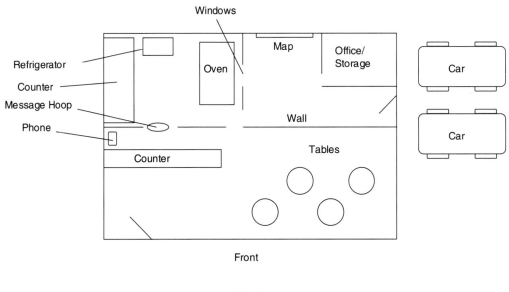

considered a fact of life, (on those occasions, the shop gives the customer the pizza for free or promises a free pizza the next time they order). The workers who answer the phones comment to you that many of the customers they get are new. Although they do not have data, they feel that they are losing a lot of long-standing, repeat customers.

You choose to understand your new business by applying the techniques of process and people system reengineering. You decide to do some homework and to do some private thinking by serving as a "one-person design team." You decide to apply the techniques yourself before involving the Pie in the Sky workers.

The Current State

These are your notes on the current operation of The Pie in the Sky Pizza Company:

• Six people work in the shop at a time. There are: 2 phone answerers, 2 pizza preparers, and 2 pizza deliverers (3 men and 3 women). The phone answerers make $6 per hour, the preparers make $10 per hour, and the deliverers make $6 per hour plus tips.

• The phone system is a five-line phone where calls roll-over to the next line if a line is busy.

• The pizza preparers prepare lumps of dough in advance, then make the pie and add the tomato sauce and ingredients when they receive an order. Normally the person who made the pizza, puts it in the oven and watches over it, although they occasionally do division-of-labor or watch out for each other's pies.

• The pizza deliverers deliver pizzas in a suburban area using their own cars and are reimbursed for mileage. There is a large map in the shop and they pinpoint their destinations before leaving.

• When a caller calls in, one of the answerers answers and asks the customer for his name. Then the answerer asks the customer for his desired size and toppings. If the Shop does not have the desired toppings, the answerer offers alternatives. If the customer agrees to the alternative suggestions, the answerer completes the order. If the customer doesn't agree, the answerer is forced to apologize and terminate the call. At the end of the call, the answerer verifies the address and form of payment (cash or check accepted).

• When the preparers receive an order (put on a circular metal hoop with clips for the paper orders filled out by the answerers), one of them prepares the pizza. Then the preparer places it in the oven to bake. After about 15 minutes (it is up to their judgment), the preparer checks the pizza. If it looks good, he takes it out. If it is not cooked enough, he allows it to bake some more. If it is overcooked, he is forced to throw away the pizza and start again (this happens just a few times per day). When the pizza is done, he boxes the pizza and places it on top of the oven to stay warm.

• When a pizza is done, one of the deliverers checks the location of the customer's address. When the deliverer gets two or three pizzas in the same area, he takes off (the deliverers do not want to leave if another pizza will be done in a minute for the same neighborhood). When they deliver the pizza, they collect the cash or check, make change for the cash if necessary (they keep $20 in change with them) and return to store. They normally earn 15-20% tips (little or none if the pizza is late or cold, much more if the pizza is for a party that is going on).

The Assignment

Process Analysis

Draw a **Current-State Relationship Map** that shows the current workflow and who does what.

Do a **Variance Analysis** of the work flow using the variance matrix or another tool.

Draw an **Ideal State Map** that shows changes you would make (if it were up to you — you have strong reason to believe that your new workers will accept you and be willing to share their ideas if you offer substantial ideas of your own).

People System Analysis

Select **three people systems** and make one recommendation in each of those categories that you feel is required by your process design or suggested by your Vision and Principles. Describe the three recommendations in enough detail that someone could pursue the specifics.

Process Thinking Glossary

A process is any activity or group of activities that takes an input, adds value to it, and provides an output to an internal or external customer.

Inputs are what enter the process and cause it to operate, including materials, information, customer requests, specifications, forms, assignments, and resources.

Outputs are the products or services produced by the process.

Customers, inside and outside, are receivers of process outputs.

Suppliers are the providers of inputs to a process.

Requirements are the expectations of clients and customers of the outputs of the process. Requirements (also called specifications) are expressed in terms of the attributes of the output to be provided.

Variability, or variation, refers to changes in the performance of the process. Some variability exists in every process.

A defect is a departure of an attribute of an output from the requirements of the client or customer.

The boundaries of a process define the start and end points of the process and the activities that produce its output. Process boundaries should allow the completion of a whole output. Hand-offs of outputs across boundaries should be smooth.

A process step is an activity within a process.

A subprocess is a set of related activities in a process.

A process owner is an individual responsible for ensuring that **the** total process is both effective and efficient.

A process stream is a set of related processes in which the outputs of one process become the inputs of the next.

Feedback is the information that tells the operators of the process how well the process is performing.

Measures are how you define the requirements of your clients in quantifiable terms.

Objectives are your performance promise. An objective captures how a requirement will be measured, and the desired level of performance for that measure.

Common cause variation is variation that is inherent to the process and thus predictable.

Special cause variation is variation that is assignable to an unpredictable, unusual cause.

References

Chapter 1

Page

5 Malcolm Forbes Jr. speaking on C-Span, March 1994.

11 Lawrence Bossidy, interview by *The Wall Street Journal*, October, 1993.

12 Marilyn R. Zuckerman and Lewis J. Hatala, *Incredibly American.* Milwaukee, Wisconsin: ASQC-Quality Press, 1992.

14 Michael Hammer, "Reengineering Work: Don't Automate, Obliterate," *Harvard Business Review*, July-August, 1990.

17 Thomas A. Stewart, *Fortune*, May 1993.

Chapter 2

30 Rosabeth Moss Kanter, *Change Masters*, Harper Business, New York, 1986.

30 Tom Peters, Video, *Liberation Management*, Video Publishing House, 1993.

31 Thomas A. Stewart, "The Search For The Organization Of Tomorrow." *Fortune*, May 18, 1992.

31 Michael Hammer and James Champy, *Reengineering The Corporation.* Harper Business, New York, 1993.

Chapter 3

42 Geary Rummler and Alan P. Brache, *Improving Performance: Managing the White Space on the Organization Chart.* Jossey-Bass, San Francisco, 1990.

54 Frank Ostroff and Doug Smith, quoted in "In Search of The Organization For Tomorrow," by Thomas A. Stewart. *Fortune,* May 18, 1992.

Chapter 4

64 Michael Hammer and James Champy, *Reengineering The Corporation*. Harper Business, New York, 1993.

Chapter 6

113 Roger Smith quote from *Forbes,* August 24, 1987.

115 Michael Hammer and James Champy, *Reengineering The Corporation*. Harper Business, New York, 1993.

Chapter 7

139 George Stalk, Jr. and Thomas M. Hout, *Competing Against Time*, Free Press, New York, 1990.

139 James Sierk, quoted in *The Wall Street Journal,* October, 1993.

Chapter 8

161 William Bridges, quoted in *USA Today*, April, 1994.

162 Charles Handy, *The Age of Paradox.* Harvard Business School Press, Boston, Massachusetts, 1994.

166 *Business Week*, Business Update on Rockwell, April, 1994.

169 Alphie Kohn, *Punished by Rewards*. Houghton Mifflin, New York, 1993.

169 Edward L. Deci, "Effects of Externally Mediated Rewards on Intrinsic Motivation." *Journal of Personality and Social Psychology,* 18 (1971), 105-15.

174 David Halberstam, *The Reckoning*. William Morrow, New York, 1986.

Chapter 9

203 J. A. Kulik, P. Jaksa, and C. L. Kulik. "Component Analysis of Personalized Instruction." *The Journal of Personalized Instruction,* Volume 3, Number 1, Spring 1978, pp. 2-14.